The Be

A Catalog of Life & Light

by BeBe

The Be Attitudes

A Catalog of Life & Light

Published by High Touch, Denver, Colorado USA
All Rights Reserved.

ISBN 978-1-59971-771-5

Library of Congress Control Number: 2007925328

Lexicon of Adjectives
Third Edition

Printed in China

www.thebeattitude.com
www.thedailyattitude.com
www.bebe.bz

1st Printing

Dear Paul

This Book Is Dedicated to…

A most incredible

"You!"

Love

Table of Contents

Introduction

As a child, I heard my parents tell me to go to my room until I changed my attitude. "What did they mean by that?" I often wondered. "What is an attitude? How can I change my attitude?" I usually found myself sitting in that room, mystified, waiting for my parents to change their attitude.

As an adult, I find that behaviors are a reflection of ones' mental approach to life, i.e. attitude. What I needed in order to behave more successfully was a wardrobe of attractive, effective and positive attitudes. I now dress my self image with attitudes chosen from the selection of optimum choices found within this menu of opportunities I call my book.

I found it's not necessarily what we think about but how we think about things that make all the difference in the world. Free the mind from the fetters of fear, which is the root of all negative attitudes by picturing positive thoughts and ideas.

Having this collection of "Be Attitudes" available to me since 1985 has greatly influenced the quality of my life. My outlook in general has improved, my relationships are more enjoyable and others find these new attitudes, attractive and infectious. It rubs off on them; and, by the way, it's wondrous to live and work... and play with people having great attitudes.

This treasury of positive words and sage advice is from the English language. Thought-provoking phrases and perceptive insight follow each "Be Attitude" for nurturing the spirit and sparking your imagination; in belief of a positive, hopeful world.

This third edition also includes dictionary definitions with each attitude as well as the "I Am" affirmation, to help promote and nurture self-validation during your reading enjoyment.

5

Fill your mind with uplifting thoughts and embark upon an inward, upward journey of well-being. Often harsh, the only fair way to gauge anyone or anything is by results. So if life isn't producing results of bliss in your every day experience then change how or what you are thinking about because "to think is to create." And, the Hallmark of a great people is.... "Life, Liberty and the Pursuit of Happiness!"

Now... step inside these attitudes. Try each on for size. Feel the part. Experience the multitude of choices available to you at any given moment. Scan through the selections often. Memorize them. Make up your own. Practice them; and, positively accept being that you are, as you choose to be.

I Wrote This Book Because...!

We use words to communicate with each other. We use words to convey concepts. Doing so helps bring order to the surrounding chaos. We command words to state our intentions and foster meanings in our relationships. In other terms – we come to words with each other and ourselves. "May I have a word with you?"

In the early 1980's I found there to be approximately 450,000 (+/-) words within the English language; I'd called the "Dictionary people" and asked them. Of this number, approximately 1300 words represent a positive, life-endorsing attitude. These attitudes are mainly descriptive words – adjectives.

Adjectives are words we use to modify nouns. Nouns are any class of words distinguished chiefly by having plural and possessive endings, and function as the subject of discussion or object of observation in a construction of a sentence, (or better yet, the fabric of thought.) Nouns designate persons, places, things, thoughts, states, times, events, feelings and qualities. We live in a conceptual world. Everything is made of mind and its' modifications. And, what so ever can be modified in one direction can always be re-modified in any other direction: as we so choose. The words we use create the stories we tell ourselves.

Section 2; "I Be I," lists more than 1300 verbs, which represent positive commands: action words. Verbs are any member of a class of words that function as the main elements of predicates, typically expressing action or state, may be inflected for tense, aspect, voice and mood, and show agreement with subject or object. A predicate is a proclamation, declaration, affirmation or assertion. "So be it!" "I am!"

One of the most fabulous features about words from the language of a culture is the un-biased aspect of the words found in that language: pre-emotionalized characters. The lexicon of a language is not political. It is not religious. It has no special interest endowment. Each word stands alone unto the cultural authority of its own meaning and shared implications. Each word alone commands the power of participation through conceptual conveyance and direction of deliberate intentional images and feelings. Each word is frequency specific.

Care in weaving words together creates amazing worlds. According to personal consent we come into agreement through our brains receiving the light of day; and then step-down trasforming that light into reality, we then watch the world reflect the intentions and probabilities we contemplate.

Although each word contains great "potential" meaning and power, words don't register in the brain until imagery meanings have been assigned and applied... until we mix these words vividly together into sentences; inherently words are still at ground zero. Therefore, great utility can be found in certain treatments of words. The treatment of The Be Attitudes, i.e. is designed to allow for, give assent to and promote positive thinking, successful being. It is the study of being; be-ology.

An ever increasing number of people are concerned with the "dumbing down" of our children... and they should be. We're giving children reputations to live down to – not up to. Violence glorified in movies and games promoting intolerance for others and other undesirable aspects of us is an inherently inferior method of rearing young.

7

In an article from the Rocky Mountain News, February 1996, Good attitude critical to health, Institute says – " An attitude adjustment is more important in preventing disease than changes in diet and exercise habits, the American Institute for Preventative Medicine says in its New Year's resolutions list."

"The No. 1 entry on the institute's sixth annual "Top Ten Healthiest Resolutions" list is to avoid psycho sclerosis" – a hardening of the attitudes," says Dr. Don Powell, president of the Detroit-based institute. "It's the way we view the events in life," he said. "We used to think physical fitness was from the neck down, but now we see it as more of an integration of mind and body."

The Be Attitudes are action triggers for formatting approaches to situations, influencing behaviors in a positive manner and providing insight and motive… or reason for participation in life itself. This is personality enhancing software.

Command action from this universe of Life and Light by using carefully chosen attitudes to describe your approach to every day living, thinking and feeling. This greatly accelerates the process of arriving at frequency specific, favorable potential realities. We modify the stories we tell ourselves about what's going on for us and thereby modify our world with what we think, say or feel about that world. "To think is to create."

Accessing and utilizing these Be Attitudes for positive results contributes to the ability of increased understanding and knowledge of mind. Knowing how to use our mind represents the extent to which we mature into the beautiful creators we are.

Learn to travel at the speed of thought and you gain knowledge of how to travel at the speed of light – the speed of love and therefore, the speed of bliss. And, why would you want to travel at the speed of bliss? Because, by traveling or vibrating at the speed of bliss you become magnetized. You become attractive. Aligning the positive in front of you and the negative behind generates a force called magnetism. Then all you need do is concentrate on that which you are attracting. Charisma!

Use The Be Attitudes as a method of positive thinking... to stretch beyond your cocoon of ordinary, everyday, comfortable considerations, and become more than what you would have been without doing so.

I created this list of positive words because "I" wanted it. I wanted to access a list, which would keep my mind occupied with all things positive, thereby promoting a blissful state of existence. Serenity! Then I wouldn't be bothered with having to keep looking at the same mundane negative crap most of us wallow around in, promoting careers in occupations of diving into the negative looking for the positive. No! Thank you!

I created this Catalog of Life and Light because I wanted to be reminded of the menu of good things life has to offer not just to balance out the bad, but also to observe the world as having infinite possibilities for non-stop good and positive things to occur. I observe that as I continue to concentrate on and appreciate - the good – that, it multiplies according to what I appreciate.

Personally, I seek to find my "bliss" as early as possible each day. I believe the world reflects what I believe it to be, so, if I were truly experiencing this belief then shouldn't I be in an ever ascending state of bliss? Am I feeling happy at this very moment? Yes! I wake up to this bliss each day and rise above even that. I live happily ever after, each and every moment that approaches.

I find bliss looks and feels differently each day I arrive. If I think bliss "should" look and feel the same each and every day... I'm sadly disappointed. That's part of the adventure – to recognize bliss in whatever forms it arrives.

I believe the standard for me to gauge anything by is by results. Does my thinking produce positively charged results? Do I enjoy the propensity to laugh? Can I bounce back from adversity and stay afloat in the sea of chaos? Am I disappointment tolerant?   Can I overcome obstacles by controlling my own attitudes? Yes! Yes! Yes!

Each time I enter traffic with my car I understand that I'm on the road with many of other people expecting certain symbols and words to mean certain things. If I think I can change meanings without regard for the consequences I won't last very long. The day is too short to be wasting it on trial and error, experimental thinking. I now live with deliberate thinking. We are designed from an incredible blueprint and imprinted within each cell of our body is the pre-eminent directive – to strive for perfection: to move toward the age of Life and Light. We respect that blueprint by unleashing the power of the intelligence that put it there in the first place... by learning how to believe.

So, as you spark your imagination by reading this book, periodically remind yourself, that there is a future you, wanting you to read this book – to become the best "you" possible. Read The Be Attitudes to your children at bedtime and let them drift off into slumber land with images worthy of their considerations. Give them options you never had when you were their age.

And finally, figure out how to get your mind to come up with this stuff on your own. This book is merely a training guide to get you to start thinking and keep you thinking – even beyond what it was designed for. Listen to your own inner voice telling you stories of how to be successful and happy. Take responsibility for what you think about and how you think about it. Mature into the fabulous person you think you are and can be... and the rest of the world will reflect this.

"The world is a mirror!

The reflectivity circuits ...are all in place!"

How To Use This Book (and Poster if you have one!)

In order to improve the world within and around you – be a role model for yourself and others. Use The Be Attitudes Book and/or Poster as a means of commanding a vast array of positive approaches to an infinite world of potential. This lexicon is a site map for that part of the English language, which lays out the realm of positive words, terms, and symbologies.

Read each Be Attitude and imagine what it's like for you to play out that particular approach to people, places, thoughts, things, events, seasons, time and other various states or stages of your life. Then as you imagine these attitudes being part of your life, so shall you poise your self within your sphere of existence.

Then as you seek... and find perfection in your personal quantum neighborhood so shall waves of infinite potential surround you and collapse into those particular particles reflecting the world you wish to see, touch and be part of.

Some tell me they use this book as an Oracle. An oracle is anything used as a medium or delivery system for sparking highly charged intelligent communication with your spirit and that of others'. While holding this book closed in your hands... close your eyes... and bring into focus, or think of, a person, place, thing, thought, state of mind or state of existence, time, event, feeling, relationship or situation in which you are needing relief, help, a solution, a benefit, or assistance. Then say to yourself... "Which attitude best applies to this situation?" "How can I best describe the most perfect scenario for all concerned?"

Then with your eyes still closed... picture a four-quadrant square in front of you. Imagine or discern which square is different or more attractive. Which square is brighter, fuzzier, softer, louder or more colorful from the rest? Is it the upper left? ... upper right? ... lower left? or, lower right?

11

Then open the book to any place... and read what it says to you within that quadrant. Read the attitude and repeat the affirmation "I am... (Blank]- whatever attitude it happens to be." Repeat the affirmation at least 16 times or, for three minutes. Then apply that attitude in action. Think about it! Contemplate it. See in your minds' eye what the outcome would look like as you apply that attitude or adopt that attitude toward that particular observation.

Repeat as needed... the whole point is to know that you always have options of approach... there is always a way – to twist a problem into a project or turn a defeat into a victory. Learn to become disappointment tolerant! Make friends with uncertainty. Illuminate doubt and it disappears.

Regarding use of the poster... (should you have one) mount the poster to the wall... hold your situation in mind then put your index finger on the poster. Then with your eyes closed... still thinking about your situation, move your finger around until you feel like stopping. Then open your eyes and see where your finger landed... which attitude is pointed out.

With this is mind, I submit the following opportunity: Survey this collection of Be Attitudes and pick out the one/s, most accurately reflecting the way you wish things to be or turn out or who you wish to become and put forth the following proposal as inspired by Dr. Joseph Dispenza, D.C. from the popular movie What The Bleep Do We Know? – (and somewhat modified by me) "I take this time to create my day, yea my life... and I infect the quantum field... which the grid of humanity is connected to... with this image of me adopting (this attitude) asking the divine observer, that is myself, to give me a sign, which, when it has done so, signals me that the quantum field has heard my request in such a manner and that I'm surprised when it does happen or appears (in my quantum neighborhood)."

What I find is myself arriving at states of bliss which tell me that I'm happy with myself and others and what better way to spend the rest of eternity than to be recognizing moments of bliss floating by on rivers of potential energy surrounding my observing brain. My identity bubble... happily floating along on this river of chaos while continually revealing goodwill and seeing the universe rewarding patience with manifestation.

Pick "Be Desirable" for instance and say, "I am desirable!" Then close your eyes and emotionalize this image. Not only picture yourself being desirable – feel it. Fire the grid!

Feel exhilarated accomplishing your goal or ascending to some other level of acquisition. Hear rounds of congratulations. The only person this matter to is you. Get real! Everyone else is doing this all the time already and is only concerned with his or her own world of potential.

So, take a deep breath, hold it for a few seconds, and then blow out. And, on the winds of your breath... picture your thoughts, these images... as being blown out into smithereens, smashed into tiny little pieces, infecting the quantum field with fragments of thoughts and desire. Then observe how they grow and multiply according to your Will.

Give thanks in advance for the time and consideration you apply to your dreams and feel grateful for your potentials. Appreciation multiplies these ideas and attracts similar thoughts, actions, people places, things, etc. Choose "Be Energetic," and say, "I am energetic!" etc. Do so each morning as you awake and repeat this in a mantra, meditative manner for at least three minutes.

The Be Attitudes are mostly adjectives, which describe or modify nouns. Use language to formulate and encapsulate your experience of being on this planet at this time among these people. Modify your world accordingly. As you modify your thinking – you modify your reality.

The whole point of these exercises is to free you from the bondage of default thinking, boring habits, unsafe addictions and erroneous superstitions... by stimulating your thoughts and sparking your imagination. Edify your belief and strengthen your faith... experience trust with enhanced confidence. Prolong your endurance in patience, bolster your tolerance with life partners and modify the psychodramas affecting you in a positive manner each and every day.

If anyone...
can be anything...
...you can!

You can do...

or be...

 ...anything!

The Be Attitudes

Be Able

Do for yourself all that you are capable of doing.
Only then will other people gladly assist you,
should you need further help.
And, as you display competence in small things,
so too will you be entrusted with larger things.
Have confidence in yourself and take those first steps.

I am able!

a*ble, *adj.* 1. having necessary power, skill, resources, or qualifications: *able to lift; able to write music; able to vote.* 2. having or showing confidence, intelligence, skill, etc.: *an able minister; an able speaker.*

Be Acting

The word "act" is the root word for the word PRACTICE.
It is the first step in making something happen.
But be advised; it is also a kindred soul of REACTION.
As you want to be a success, act like you're successful.

I am acting!

act*ing *adj.* 1. doing something; exerting energy or force; being employed or operative. 2. reaching, making, or issuing a decision on some matter. 3. operating, functioning, or serving in a particular way: *acting chairman.* 4. producing an effect; performing a function. 5. behaving or conducting oneself in a particular fashion: *acting well under all conditions.* 6. performing on a stage as an actor or an actress.

15

Be Adept

Seek to be first-rate with your abilities.
Obtain first rate results from emotionalized contemplations.
Promote proficiency with time and energy.
Cultivate a refined sense for your abilities.
Command the English language
with confidence in your skills and talents.
As Benjamin Franklin inspires,
"Be a jack of all trades... and master of most!"

I am adept!

ad*ept *adj.* very skilled; proficient; expert.

Be Aerobic

Inspire! Take a deep breath, through your nose. Hold it.
Now exhale by blowing out
through a tiny hole through pursed lips.
Repeat as many times as you can.
FInd comfort riding on the inhale side of each breath cycle;
pressurize the exhale side of breathing.
Cancer and numerous bacteria and viruses
are anaerobic life forms
and cannot exist in an atmosphere filled with oxygen.
Anxiety has roots in the Greek language meaning,
"excitement without breath."
Stop holding your stomach in.
Use your diaphragm.

I feel aerobic... I am aerobic.

aer*o*bic *adj.* 1. (*of an organism or tissue*) requiring air or free oxygen for life.
2. pertaining to or caused by the presence of oxygen. 3. of or utilizing the
principles of aerobics: *aerobic dancing.*

Be Aesthetic

Variety is essential to the concept of beauty.
Take the contrasts you find in life
and unify them with your sense of harmony.
Promote the artistic side of yourself
and seek splendor in everyday living.
Enjoy a refined sense of taste... and ...
glimmer your buds to life... with light... in all its forms.

I feel aesthetic...

I am aesthetic!

aes*thet*ic *adj.* 1. pertaining to a sense of the beautiful or to aesthetics. 2. having a sense of the beautiful or characterized by a love of beauty. 3. pertaining to, involving, or concerned with pure emotion and sensation as opposed to pure intellectuality.

Be Affable

Be likeable to yourself first,
then watch others respond accordingly.
Seek out thoughts and things,
which are beautiful and worthy of observation.
The presence of a friend enhances enjoyment of living,
promotes good will and powerful intentions.
Seize each day inviting friends to share affinities with each other.

I feel affable... I... am affable!

aff*fa*ble *adj.* 1. pleasantly easy to talk to; cordial. 2. showing warmth and friendliness. – *syn.* amiable, courteous.

Be Affectionate

Touch each other in a loving manner.
Continue to attend to relationships
with sincere, heartfelt endearments.
Tenderly care for those you love.
Show loved ones how much you think and feel about them;
tell them, then listen.

I feel affectionate...

I am affectionate!

af*fec*tion*ate *adj.* 1. showing or characterized by affection or tenderness.
2. having great affection or love.

Be Affluent

Observe abundance all around you.
Show others how to reach... for the potential available.
Let the garden of life you're cultivating
represent an estate worth building.
Not only have wealth but use wealth to promote wealth.
It's not enough that you're the only one happy and prosperous.
Let physical, mental and spiritual possibilities... flourish.

I feel affluent...

I... am affluent.

af*flu*ent *adj.* 1. prosperous; wealthy. 2. abounding in anything; abundant.
3. conditioned by or based on prosperity or wealth: *an affluent society.* 4. flowing
freely.

Be Ageless

Take your time today; life isn't a race.
Don't restrict yourself to a calendar or chronological age.
You have the rest of eternity to become who you are.
Flow easily amid the endless pace
of this forever river of moments.
Slip into time without end... by pronouncing the "I Am..."
Impatience is poison to the spirit.
When your spirit is sick it cannot enjoy bliss.
Live in the ever-present here & now as blissfully as possible.

I feel ageless...

I am ageless!

age*less *adj.* never growing old or outdated.

Be Alluring

Let the essence of you come forth
and disclose irresistible appeal.
Arouse magnetic fascination
with an attractively charming personality.
Let sight, sound, aroma and touch entice the apple of your eye.
Allow the moan of awe... that you have for life,
to be heard loud and clear.

I... am alluring!

al*lur*ing *adj.* 1. tempting; enticing. 2. fascinating; charming.

Be Altruistic

Feel thankful for those who dedicated their lives...
so you could have a better chance in life...
than they had... when they were born.
Always be concerned with the welfare of our children's children.
Do things now because they need to be done,
not necessarily because you're paid to do so.
Appreciate rewards found in thoughts and actions...
given in consideration of... being first to give.

I feel like being altruistic...

I am altruistic!

al*tru*is*tic *adj.* unselfishly concerned for or devoted to the welfare of others.

Be Amazed

Receive delight in all you find awe-inspiring.
Observe this world through the eyes of the inner child.
Marvel at the breathless wonders of Life and Light
within this vast universe we live.
Enjoy surprises you feel...
upon finding answers or solutions you seek.
Feel delighted upon finding truth, beauty and goodness
everywhere you go.

I am amazed!

a*mazed *adj.* filled with wonder; astounded.

Be Ambitious

Be eager... and bold...
to unleash the power of reaching for your dreams.
Don't settle for anything less than what you desire.
Experience emotional passion for enthusiasm
luring chests of treasures... towards you.
Life is yours for the taking;
"So what are you waiting for? – Grab it!"

I feel ambitious... I am ambitious!

am*bi-tious *adj.* 1. having ambition; eagerly desirous of achieving or obtaining power; superiority, or distinction: *ambitious students*. 2. showing or caused by ambition. 3. requiring exceptional effort, ability. etc. – *syn.* AMBITIOUS, ENTERPRISING, ASPIRING describes a person who wishes to rise above his or her present position or condition. The AMBITIOUS person wishes to attain worldly success and puts forth effort toward this end: ambitious for social position. The ENTERPRISING person, interested especially in financial wealth, is characterized by energy and daring in undertaking projects. The ASPIRING person wishes to rise (mentally and/or spiritually) to a higher level or plane; to attain an end they feel is above ordinary expectations or station in life.

Be Amiable

Remain affectionate with those in your inner circle.
Feel easygoing with your mate... as well as with friends.
Allow your sensibilities with strangers to be genteel.
Seek to create an atmosphere of friendly exchanges.
Playfully express... deep meanings... in personal relation-ships.
Promote the positive similarities you have with others.

I feel amiable... I am amiable!

a*mi*a*ble *adj.* 1. having or showing a friendly, willing disposition. 2. free of rancor, as a contest or discussion. – *syn.* gracious; amicable.

21

Be Amusing

Emanate the gentle, lightness of life.
Elicit happiness with laughter and good-cheer,
pleasantly and unexpectedly, bringing joy to yourself and others.
Find humor in your inner dialog...
and ongoing personal relationships.
Cause others to know genuine laughter
and good times when you're around.

I feel... amusing...   I am... amusing!

a*mus*ing *adj.* 1. pleasantly entertaining or diverting. 2. exciting laughter or gentle mirth; delighting the fancy. – *syn.* 1. charming, cheering, lively, laughable, delightful, funny. 2. AMUSING, COMICAL, DROLL describe that which causes mirth. That which is AMUSING is quietly humorous or funny in a gentle, good-humored way: *The baby's attempts to talk were amusing.* That which is COMICAL causes laughter by being incongruous, witty, or ludicrous: His huge shoes made the clown look comical. DROLL adds to COMICAL the idea of strange or peculiar, and sometimes that of sly or waggish humor: *droll antics of a kitten, a droll imitation.*

Be Appealing

Promote that which has real, vivid and eternal value within you.
Garnish your attractiveness with truth, beauty and goodness.
Display fashion sense with a style appropriate to your body,
and decorate your mind with feelings of optimistic gladness...
for being alive, attaining your goals and reaching your dreams.
Life is your runway;
carry yourself with poise and dynamic self-evident presence.

I... am appealing!

ap*peal*ing *adj.* evoking or attracting interest, desire, curiosity, sympathy, or the like; attractive.

Be Appreciative

That to which you feel and show admiration for...
multiplies and grows more valuable over time.
Develop the mental muscle of appreciation
by escalating the value of your considerations
deepening life's meanings felt thereby.
Attend to feelings of gratitude
and let bliss expand your capacity for appreciation.
After you can do this, start commanding the Law of Attraction.
Realize that by emulating positive attitudes and approaches
you'll start feeling results of those viewpoints and appreciations.
What once started out as an acorn...
ends up being the mighty oak.

I feel appreciative... I am appreciative!

ap*pre*cia*tive *adj.* 1. feeling or showing appreciation. 2. capable of appreciation; enjoyment. 3. magnifying; magnificent. (*Ed. Note.* Law of Attraction, where thoughts become things, which is as powerful and certain as the Law of Gravity.)

Be Approachable

Be easy to talk with and pleasant to know.
Allow your unfolding personality to be accessible
with all of its emotions and intelligence.
Smile to signal others that you are present...
and feel open for business.
Imagine many people coming to you for advice... and company
because they feel... you're ready, willing and able.

I feel approachable... I am approachable!

ap*proach*a*ble *adj.* 1. capable of being approached; accessible. 2. (*of a person*) easy to talk with or straightforward to know.

Be Articulate

Present your ideas with clarity.
Learn to use languages easily and fluently.
Enunciate each word clearly and promote understanding.
Formulate your thoughts precisely
and speak your mind effectively.
Periodically pause long enough... to take a deep breath ...
and avoid using filler words like um, ah ...
'ermm and... d'ja know what I mean?
Do you want to axe me a question... or ask me a question?

I am articulate!

ar*tic*u*late *adj.* 1. uttered clearly in distinct syllables. 2. capable of speech.
3. using language easily and fluently; having facility with words: *an articulate
person.* 4. expressive; formulative, or presented with clarity and effectiveness:
an articulate speech. 5. clear, distinct, and precise in relation to other parts: *an
articulate form.* 6. organized into a coherent or meaningful whole: *an articulate
system of philosophy.*

Be Artistic

Creatively add depth felt to perception of meaning
and breadth of observation to perspective.
Paint the canvas of your Life and Light
with the brushes of truth, beauty and goodness.
Show skill and excellence in all your art forms...
whatever they may be.
Produce eye candy, ear candy, mind candy and spirit candy
for amusement and entertainment of yourself... as well as others.

I feel artistic... I am artistic!

ar*tis*tic *adj.* 1. conforming to the standards of art; satisfying aesthetic
requirements. 2. showing skill or excellence in execution. 3. exhibiting taste,
discriminating judgment, or sensitivity. 4. of, or pertaining to, the appreciation of
art: *artistic interests.*

Be Asking

It isn't dumb to ask questions,
but it would be dumb if you didn't.
Don't be afraid to ask.
Make your requests known!
Everyone does!

I am asking!

I feel like asking... I ask!

ask*ing *adj.* 1. putting a question to; inquire of: *I'm asking him.* 2. requesting information about: to be asking the way. 3. to try to get by using words; request: to ask a favor; to ask for advice. 4. to demand, expect, or desire: *What price are they asking? A little silence is all I'm asking.* 5. to call for; require: *This experiment is asking for patience.* 6. inviting: *to be asking guests to dinner.*

Be Assertive

Honestly promote your opinions and your actions
by placing your footing on the firm ground of your self-esteem.
Act in ways which enhance your self-respect...
and watch others respond accordingly.
Put your best foot forward because there are gains to be made.
If anyone can do whatever, you can!

I feel assertive...

I am assertive!

as*ser*tive *adj.* given to asserting; positive or aggressive: *They're quite assertive in their program presentation.*

Be Assisting

Be present in your life
by giving support and aid when someone else needs it.
Don't just give lip service;
roll up your sleeves and help be of service.
It takes both a crew and a crowd to put on a concert
and collective effort to build an estate.
Be available physically, emotionally, mentally and spiritually.

I feel like assisting...

I am assisting!

as*sist*ing *adj.* 1. giving support or aid to; helping. 2. associating with as an
assistant. 3. serving in an immediately subordinate position: *an assisting manager.*

Be Attentive

Attention is a magnificent mental energy force.
The success of your intentions
depends on your ability to use this magnifying energy.
"Focus it!"
Like a musicians' instrument,
perspective is a finely tuned tool
for practicing conscious perception.
"Tune it!"
Attention:
concentration, is "the" mental energy force to use...
in today's world.

I am attentive!

at*ten*tive *adj.* 1. characterized by or giving attention; observant. 2. thoughtful of
others; considerate; polite; courteous: *she is very attentive to her guests.*
3. directing the focus of the mind to an object of thought.

Be Attractive

Produce feelings of pleasure
and delight for yourself and those around you
by being present
with beauty vibrating appeal for a loved one.
Aesthetic forms and inspiring ideas
decorate body, mind and spirit
according to your appreciation and considerations of quality.
You are most attractive... when you are simply being yourself.

I feel attractive...

I am attractive!

at*trac*tive *adj.* 1. appealing to one's sense of beauty; providing pleasure or delight, esp. in appearance or manner; pleasing; charming; alluring: *an attractive man or woman.* 2. arousing interest or engaging one's thought, consideration, etc.: *an attractive idea.* 3. having the quality of attracting.

Be Authentic

Be genuine and real...
and others will treat you as reliable and trustworthy.
Your alignment with known facts and experience
entitles you to acceptance and belief.
Imagine filling in and filing a patent application
for blueprint designs called "you."
The life span of this deed will be for eternity
so, stake your claim for this original work of art.

I feel authentic...

I am authentic!

au*then*tic *adj.* 1. entitled to acceptance or belief because of agreement with known facts or experience; reliable; trustworthy: an authentic portrayal of the past. 2. not false or copied; genuine; real: *an authentic antique.*

Be Autonomous

The one who conquers self has conquered the world.
If you don't choose to do this... others will do it for you.
Operate under your own will power.
Have courage to believe in your dreams
... and move freely about the cabin of your life.
Enjoy liberty because it is the next step in your evolution.
Autonomy is a feature free men and women appreciate
in a free society.

I feel autonomous...

I am autonomous!

au*ton*o*mous *adj.* 1. self-governing. 2. of, or pertaining to, a self-governing or independent state, community, organization, etc.

Be Available

Feel suitable and ready for use.
Be present in mind for yourself and others.
Feel accessible emotionally, so life is not a lonely journey.
Participate in all the reindeer games.

I feel available...

I am available!

a*vail*a*ble *adj.* 1. suitable or ready for use; usable; at hand: *he used whatever excuse seemed available.* 2. readily obtainable; accessible: *available resources.* 3. having sufficient power or efficacy; valid. 4. plausible.

Be Aware

Consciously acknowledge your life and make the best of it.
Conquer feelings of fear by becoming familiar with
the function and effects of courage.
Watch each dawn arrive with a new sureness of success
and dynamic feelings of positivity
helping you see the way things are and can be
versus how they only seem to be.
Be mindful and knowledgeable, ready to respond
to the known and the unknown.

I feel aware...

I am aware!

a*ware *adj.* 1. having knowledge; conscious; cognizant: *aware of the danger.*
2. informed; alert; knowledgeable: *He is one of the most politically aware young men around.*

Be Balanced

Great peace of mind, i.e. serenity, can be attained
when perspective has been adjusted to harmonious proportions.
Stability is an ever-changing series of events, however,
so remain ready to make adjustments
with tolerance, moderation and approach.
Peripheral perception and equilibrium is enhanced
by this insight.

I feel balanced...

I am balanced!

bal*anced *adj.* being in harmonious or proper arrangement or adjustment, proportion.

Be Beatific

Exist in the bliss of happiness and sublime satisfaction.
Use the scope of your vision to get pleasure
from the blessed awareness of simply "being" here now.
Appreciate the side-effects of serenity, peace, and joy.
Participate in unfolding gardens of love
with a taste for the spiritual life.
Be delighted, felicitous and hopeful.

I feel beatific... I am beatific!

be*a*tif*ic *adj.* 1. bestowing bliss, blessings, happiness, or the like: *a period of beatific peace.* 2. blissful; saintly: *a beatific smile.*

Be Beautiful

That which is beautiful
has excellence of form, color and presence.
Beauty includes the noble and spiritual qualities
of you... being you, to the fullest.
Have pleasingly attractive effects upon those around you.
Let feelings of happiness within you reflect the goodness of truth,
the truth of beauty and the beauty of goodness.

I feel beautiful... I am beautiful!

beau*ti*ful *adj.* 1. having beauty; delighting the senses of mind. 2. excellent of its kind: *a beautiful putt on the seventh hole.* 3. wonderful; very pleasing or satisfying. – *syn.* 1. comely, seemly, attractive. 2. BEAUTIFUL, HANDSOME, LOVELY, PRETTY refer to a pleasing appearance. That which is BEAUTIFUL has perfection of form, color, etc., or noble and spiritual qualities: *a beautiful landscape, girl or woman (seldom man.)* HANDSOME often implies stateliness or pleasing proportion and symmetry: *a handsome man (seldom woman.)* That which is LOVELY is beautiful but in a warm and endearing way: *a lovely smile.* PRETTY implies a moderate but noticeable beauty, especially in that which is petite, i.e. on the very slender side.

Be Being

Be a human being, not just a human doing or a human having.
Possess and feel the essence of personal presence.
Experience the multitude of attitudinal choices available to you
within the currently surrounding kingdom of "Being!"
Relationships, adventures and activities of body, mind and spirit
fill your waking hours as the river of time continues flowing by
moment by moment, day after day... after day.

I feel like being...

I am being!

be*ing *v. i.* 1. to exist or live. 2. to take place; occur: *The wedding is this week.*
3. to occupy a place or position: *The book is on the table.* 4. to continue or
remain as before: *Let it be.* 5. to belong; attend; befall: *Good fortune is being
with you.* – *n.* 1. the fact of existence as opposed to nonexistence. 2. conscious,
mortal existence; life. 3. substance or nature: *of such a being as to arouse fear.*
4. something that exists: *inanimate beings.* 5. a living thing: *strange exotic beings
that live in the depths of the sea.* 6. a human being; person. *adj.* 1. the action of
doing something. 2. participating as: *just being me.*

Be Believing

Believing is the art of commanding the attitudes you adopt
toward the content of your thinking, feeling and appreciation.
Have confidence the truth within will always ring true.
And, as you shine the light of faith and intelligence,
the truth will indeed set you free.

I am believing!

be*liev*ing *adj.* 1. having confidence in the truth or the reliability of something
without absolute proof. 2. having confidence or faith in the reality of (*a positive
assertion, story, etc.*) 3. having confidence in the statement or assertion of
(*a person.*)

31

Be Benevolent

Do good or cause good to be done.
Be tender and loving in action and purpose.
"Volant" means voluntary and "bene" means good.
Be voluntarily good.
Those who truly have, can give, and more will be given them,
and those who don't believe they have,
end up never truly having had.
You are not your brother/sisters' keeper;
you **are** your brother/sister.

I feel benevolent...

I am benevolent!

be*nev*o*lent, *adj.* 1. desiring to do good to others: *gifts from several benevolent alumni*. 2. intended for benefits rather than profit: *a benevolent institution.* 3. characterized by good will: *a benevolent attitude.* – *syn.* generous, benign, charitable: *the benevolent man brought the envelope to the orphanage.*

Be Better

You don't have to be sick to get better,
because there is always room for improvement.
Periodically upgrade your personality enhancement software.
Remember, be not better than, just... better.
Don't lord your virtues over others.
Improve yourself because you can, not because you have to.

I am... better!

bet*ter *adj.* 1. of superior quality or excellence: *a better coat.* 2. morally superior; more virtuous: *He's no better than a thief!* 3. of superior value, use fitness, desirability, acceptableness: *a better time for action.* 4. larger; greater: *the better part of a lifetime.* 5. improved in health; healthier: *Is your mother better?*

Be Blessed

Be blissfully happy and contented,
knowing that you are worthy of being happy.
You not only have faculties for being blessed
you have personal prerogative to be so.
You were creatively designed to be this way;
it's in your blueprint.
Live... in bliss.

I feel blessed...

I am blessed!

bless*ed *adj.* 1. consecrated; sacred; holy; sanctified. 2. worthy of adoration, reverence. 3. divinely or supremely favored; fortunate: *to be blessed with a healthy body.* 4. blissfully happy or contented: *living a blessed life; a charmed existence.*

Be Blooming

Unfold in your life like a flower.
Allow yourself to establish your roots; find nourishment.
Create the structure of your stem,
send forth leaves to receive light,
blossom exuberantly with the colors of your petals
and (in other words) smile!

I... am blooming!

bloom*ing *adj.* 1. in bloom; flowering; blossoming. 2. glowing, as with youthful vigor and freshness: *blooming cheeks.* 3. flourishing; prospering: *a blooming business.*

Be Bountiful

Now is the season for giving and receiving.
Recognize the lavish banquet of life surrounding you
and lead others to it in gratitude.
Through you,
experience the cornucopia of the fruits of the spirit
offered by Life and Light.
There is more than enough food for everybody.
There are more than enough jobs for everyone.
There are more than enough resources for everyone.
There are ample supplies of energy
for on and on... beyond the Ages of Life and Light.

I feel bountiful... I am bountiful!

boun*ti*ful *adj.* 1. liberal in bestowing gifts, favors, or bounties; munificent;
generous. 2. abundant; ample: *a bountiful supply.*

Be Brain-Storming

Put your heads together.
Develop new ideas with others.
Participate in solving problems and designing projects
with unrestrained discussions.
Use counsel with your associates to obtain
a birds eye view of your ventures.
Stick your neck out and speak up;
your ideas are worthy of being heard,
and, even if they aren't,
at least you'll have said what others are too chicken to say.

I feel like brain-storming...
I am brain-storming!

brain*storm*ing *verb.* a conference technique of solving specific problems,
developing new ideas, etc., by unrestrained participation in discussion.
– *adj.* someone who practices brainstorming.

Be Brave

Courage is the ability to act upon ideas, intuition and feelings.
Bravery is simply being willing
to believe in purpose and take action.
Become what you dream about, go where you dare.
Say what needs to be said and feel what needs to be cared for.
Qualify liberty as a means for free-will
to express appreciation for paradise perfection.

I feel brave... I am brave.

brave *adj*. 1. possessing or exhibiting courage or courageous endurance.
2. making a fine appearance. 3. *Archaic*. excellent; fine; admirable.

Be Bright

Be animated, lively and cheerful.
First look to the light as the source of your being,
and as you do so others will see it, too.
You reflect that which you concentrate on.
Polish yourself into a brilliant personality.

I am bright!

bright *adj*. 1. radiating or reflecting much light; luminous; shining. 2. filled with
light. 3. vivid or brilliant. 4. clear or translucent, as liquid. 5. radiant or splendid:
the bright pageantry of court. 6. illustrious or glorious, as an era. 7. quick-witted or
intelligent. 8. showing quick wit or intelligence. 9. favorable or auspicious: *bright
prospects.* 10. having a glossy, glazed, or polished finish.

Be Brilliant

Take command of your talents
and magnify them with joyous, blissful participation.
The power of an idea
lay not so much in how valid or reasonable it is,
but how vivid and story-like you can make it.
Don't just tell others what you're going to do:
show them what you've done, can do or are already doing.
Be on top of your game
and in the flow of who you believe you already are.

I feel brilliant... I am brilliant!

bril*liant *adj.* 1. shining brightly; sparkling; glittering; lustrous. 2. distinguished;
illustrious. 3. having or showing great intelligence or talent.

Be Buoyant

In the great ocean of life,
allow yourself to always rise to the surface.
Bounce back from feeling depression caused by disappointments
and regain your posture.
Learn to become disappointment tolerant.
Within each day are new opportunities
for making new things happen.
You can do it... bounce back!
Let bliss inflate your self-esteem.

I feel buoyant... I am buoyant!

boi*yant *adj.* 1. tending to float or rise in a fluid. 2. capable of, or keeping an object
afloat, as a liquid. 3. cheerful. 4. cheering or invigorating.

Be Calm

Move serenely through your world
and give permission for a tranquil solution to life's problems.
Be a mirror for others, for through you,
they too gain a greater presence... of peace of mind.
Your ability to remain calm
provides a reflecting pool for the angry
so when they become (inevitably) exhausted
from thrashing about in their futilities
they can perhaps then see themselves
and change, should they so choose.

I feel calm... I... am calm!

calm *adj.* 1. without rough motion; still or nearly still: *a calm sea.* 2. not windy:
a calm day. 3. free from excitement of passion; tranquil: *a calm face; a calm
manner; a calm force; a calm spirit.*

Be Candid

Remain open in your heart and mind, sincere in your feelings
and spontaneous in your observations and remarks.
Give permission for your affairs to be filled
with heart-to-heart exchanges of genuine humor.
Let laughter roll off the tip of your tongue
and pursue the playful pleasures of like minds.
Recognize commonplace, funny situations as they appear.
However, avoid belittling others
because that's only a bad reflection on you!
Stay on the fun side of life.

I feel candid... I am candid!

can*did *adj.* 1. frank; outspoken; open and sincere: *a candid reply.* 2. without
reservation, disguise, or subterfuge; straightforward: *a candid opinion.* 3. informal;
unposed: *a candid photo.* 4. honest; impartial: *a candid mind.*

Be Cause

Be the cause for something, not just the effect.
Choose to be the master of your destiny
and captain of your ship.
With a map, a plan, and a reason why you feel you must,
you can go around the world and beyond our galaxy.
Cause... is the first half of this "cause and effect" universe.

I am cause!

cause *n.* 1. a person or thing that acts, happens, or exists in such a way that some specific thing happens as a result; the producer of an effect: *You have been the cause of much excitement. What is the cause of this celebration?* 2. the reason or motive for some human action: *This news was a cause for great rejoicing.*

Be Centered

Have a healthy approach to daily life.
Drive each day as from the middle of your bliss.
Be fueled with perspectives,
which balance good out front and bad far behind.
You can easily reach more points of interest
as you remain equidistant from them.
Stay calm and pilot your life vehicle with precision.

I am centered!

cen*tered *n.* 1. the middle point as the point within a circle or sphere equally distant from all points of the circumference or surface. 2. a pivot, point, axis, etc. around which anything rotates or revolves. 3. the source of an influence, action, force, etc.: *centered within a project.* 4. a point, place, person, etc., upon which interest, emotion, etc. focuses: *She was centered as the highlight of the party.* 5. the part of a legislative assembly, holding political views intermediate between Right and Left: *He was strong enough in his opinions to be centered on the issues.* – *adj.* center of thought/s, feeling/s and thing/s. Mahatma Gandhi reminds us, *"Each man and woman is the center of a circle, which has no circumference."*

Be Certain

Let intuition lead to understanding...
then have courage to know... you know what you know.
Be free from feelings of doubt and reservation.
Recognize... that which you passionately want
in your heart is truly possible.
Become aware also, that you will eventually learn
how to become sublimely uncertain,
because the future is always in motion
within this space-time continuum.

I feel certain... I am certain!

cer*tain *adj.* 1. destined; sure (*usually followed by an infinitive*): *He is certain to be there.* 2. inevitable; bound to happen: *They realized then that peace was certain.* 3. established as true or sure; unquestionable: *It is certain that he tried.* 4. fixed; agreed upon: *one certain day; for a certain amount.* 5. definite or particular, but not named or specified: *a certain person; a certain charm.* 6. that may be depended on; trustworthy.

Be Changing

Attend the present with an aptitude
for modifying your world and your identity
toward a desirable future.
If you don't like the way something is,
then it's your responsibility to change it.
What you are becoming is much more important to dwell on
than what you appear to be... right now.
Pursue self-directed re-construction for the right reasons;
because **you** want to.

I feel like changing... I am changing!

chang*ing *adj.* 1. making different the form, nature, content, future course, etc., of (*something*). 2. transforming or converting (*usually followed by into*): *The witch is changing the toad into a prince?* 3. substituting another or others for; exchanging for something else, usually of the same kind.

Be Charismatic

Exercise a remarkable drawing power over people
without dictatorship.
Inspire hope and feelings of confidence
in the hearts of those you encounter.
When in a room of negative people, start talking.
Darkness cannot exist in the presence of light.

I feel charismatic... I am charismatic!

cha*ris*ma*tic *adj.* 1. exhibiting a divinely conferred gift or power. 2. a special
quality that gives an individual influence or authority over large numbers of people.
3. the special virtue of an office, position, etc. that confers or is thought to confer
on the person holding it an unusual ability for leadership, worthiness or veneration,
admiration or the like.

Be Cheerful

Promote cheer by being cheerful.
Express happiness within the sphere of your personal existence.
Induce a pleasant mirth when you're by yourself...
or with others.
Embody a hearty inclination to work happily,
with feelings of optimism.
Feeling good(ness)... cheers every cell of your body.
Convince yourself that cheer is a feeling,
excellent to enjoy most of the time.
Others will come to know you
as that uncompromisingly cheerful person.

I feel cheerful...

I am cheerful!

cheer*ful *adj.* 1. full of cheer; in good spirits. 2. promoting, inducing, or expressing
cheer; pleasant; bright: *cheerful surroundings.* 3. hearty or ungrudging: *cheerful
giving.* 4. gruntled (*as in able to grunt or hum*): *cheerful tones of voice.*

Be Clear

Leave fogginess of thinking behind
by learning to focus your mind.
Zoom in or zoom out on this matter... or that.
Speak your mind clearly and with knowledgeable intent.
Feeling good indicates the extent of how clear you are.
Lift the veil of uncertainty and be convinced.

I feel clear...

I... am clear!

clear *adj.* 1. free from darkness, obscurity, or cloudiness: *a clear day.* 2. bright; shinning: *a clear flame.* 3. easily understood; without ambiguity: *clear concise answers.* 4. entirely comprehensible; completely understood: *The ultimate causes of war may never be clear, but its effects will some day clear up.*

Be Clever

Show inventiveness with daily routines
and originality in your intentions.
Feel mentally bright and utilize your intelligence.
Become familiar with the Source and it's re-Sources.
Be skillful in adopting your traits and characteristics.

I am... clever!

clev*er *adj.* 1. mentally bright; having quick intelligence; able. 2. superficially skillful, witty, or original in character or construction; facile: *her project shows how clever she is.* 3. adroit with the hands or body; dexterous or nimble. 4. showing inventiveness or originality; ingenious.

Be Cohesive

Be a force within the soul of humanity,
which acts to unify its parts.
Inspire others to work together by vocalizing desired end results.
People act or react according
to what attracts them or repels them:
discern which one motivates your audience;
use this insight as the operating glue
for family, personnel management and marketing plans.
Move cohesively within the story lines of your aspirations.

I feel cohesive...

I am cohesive!

co*he*sive *adj.* 1. characterized by or causing cohesion: *a cohesive agent.*
2. cohering; tending to stick together; hold fast, as parts of the same mass:
a cohesive organization. 3. of, or pertaining to, the molecular magnetic force within
a body or substance acting to unite its parts.

Be Colorful

Be rich in impulse and when you view dramatic scenarios of life,
let your imagination make the best of things... just because.
Display the rainbow-like spectrum of your personal attributes
when dealing with others.
As an artist blends color, bend the light.
Flavor comments and contributions
with the spices of your personality.

I feel like being colorful...

I'm colorful!

col*or*ful *adj.* 1. abounding in color. 2. richly picturesque: *a colorful historical
period.* 3. full of vivid or distinctive qualities: *his home is quite colorful.* 4. the
natural appearance of the skin, especially of the face: *She's quite colorful.*

Be Comforting

Soothe and console the people you care about.
Encourage them beyond difficult passing moments.
Think of ways to help them
do things they cannot do for themselves.
Comforting someone...
doesn't mean you're adopting their problems,
it simply means you're reminding them to not be or feel alone.

I feel comforting...

I am comforting!

com*fort*ing *adj.* 1. affording comfort. 2. allowing physical comfort. 3. producing mental comfort or ease: *the nurse was very comforting.*

Be Comical

Promote truly excellent causes and genuine reasons
for laughing to tears.
Be willing to be so humble... that you can laugh at yourself,
and allow others to do so as well.
You know you're in the company of friends
as laughter is being heard.
Relaxation and healing
are two of the many positive side-effects of laughter.
Relief from the stress of being serious
promotes the creation of bliss.

I feel comical...

I am comical!

com*i*cal *adj.* 1. producing laughter; amusing; funny. 2. pertaining to, or of the nature of, comedy: *Their comical disturbance wasn't appreciated in class.*

Be Committed

Entrust yourself to that which is worthy of you.
Empower your relationships
with assurance of believable intentions.
Awaken daily with similar resolve;
with similar feelings of insight, motivation and convictions
you went to bed with the previous night.
Be willing to get behind a project or relationship
and see it through to fruition.

 I feel committed...

I am committed!

com*mit*ted *adj.* 1. given in trust or charge; consigned. 2. relegated for preservation: committed to memory. 3. delivered to custody; to commit a delinquent to a reformatory school. 4. pledged or devoted (*oneself*) to a position on an issue, question, project or program: *they committed their lives to their ten children.*

Be Compassionate

Your grasp of empathy desires relief;
removal of the cause for pain and suffering,
for yourself as well as others.
Compassion emanates when you act on this desire.
Originating from passion,
this attitude helps liquefy contact with life.
As you act as an angel for others, angels will show up for you.

I feel compassionate...

I am compassionate!

com*pas*sion*ate *adj.* having or showing a feeling of deep sympathy and sorrow for the suffering or misfortune of another, accompanied by a desire to alleviate pain or help remove its cause.

Be Complimentary

Life is what you make of it.
Make it good.
Not good and bad.
Just... good!
And, as you express your insights and opinions to others,
commend your listeners constructively
and foster their self-esteem
in ways you would for yourself.
Let your light shine positively on the attributes of Life and Light
and feel good about each other's presence.

I am complimentary!

com*pli*men*ta*ry *adj.* 1. of the nature of, conveying, or expressing a compliment,
often one that is politely flattering: *complimentary reviews of his novel;
a complimentary remark.* 2. expressing praise, commendation, or admiration.
3. to congratulate or felicitate.

Be Confident

Believe in yourself.
Feel assured that you are standing on the firm ground
of understanding how manifestation occurs.
Know that you know...
and feel connected...
with the knowledge library-bank built upon experience.
Give yourself permission to be bold
and exhibit courage in the face of uncertainty.
Have faith your dreams are on their way of becoming true!

I feel confident... I am confident!

con*fi*dent *adj.* 1. having strong belief or full assurance; sure. 2. certain of oneself;
bold: *a confident speaker.* 3. trustful and confiding.

Be Conscientious

Have a feeling for a sense of what is right or not-so-right
in conduct and motive,
impelling you toward worthy decisions, effective action
and consequences you can live with.
Con-scious means "with-thought."
Con-scientious means "with-scientific-thought."
Come the dawn... all thoughts and things are brought to light.
Expand your capacity for appreciation.

I am conscientious!

con*sci*en*tious *adj.* 1. controlled by or done according to moral or ethical
principles that control or inhibit the actions or thoughts of an individual.
2. meticulous; careful.

Be Conscious

Be "with thought,"
aware of what you are being, doing, having, and saying,
sensitive to the stories you hear and tell yourself.
Pay attention;
notice to where and when you direct your attention.
Be personally present in your observations,
of thinking... and feeling... and interacting with others.
Be here and feel now!

I am conscious!

con*scious *adj.* 1. aware of one's own existence, thoughts, surroundings, etc.
2. fully aware of, or sensitive to, something (*often followed by of*): *conscious of
one's own faults and virtues.* 3. having the mental faculties fully active: *He was not
conscious during the operation; She is conscious of her appearance.*

Be Considerate

Be so strong that you can put others first.
Assume a perspective or point of view
that considers all five* sides of a coin.
Deliberately contemplate and have regard for
other people's feelings and circumstances.
As you reach for thoughts and things,
make them available for the next person passing.
Hold doors open for others
and encourage others to do the same.

I feel considerate...

I am considerate!

con*sid*er*ate *adj.* 1. having regard for another's feelings, circumstances, etc.
2. carefully considering; deliberate. (*Ed. Note.* - five sides of a coin, 1) top side,
2) other, bottom side 3) the side, side, 4) the inside and 5) the outside.)

Be Consistent

Steadfastly adhere to integrated principles and motives.
Repeated courses of action (habits)
form structure for thought and feeling.
Maintain demand for quality today as well as tomorrow.
Find the right formula
and stabilize production for quantity of quality.
Preserve passing rivers of moments
by continuing to enjoy peace... in presence of mind.

I am consistent!

con*sist*ent *adj.* 1. not self-contradictory. 2. holding firmly together; cohering.

Be Consoling

Help lessen other people's feelings
of grief, sorrow and disappointment.
Re-establish a sense of solace and hope
by relating their personal story
to another's story of survival and success.
Reach for those caught in quick sands of despair and depression
and offer to pull them out...
with the lifeline of your caring thoughts and actions.
Explain grief to be an accessory of loving someone.
Nurture and help heal their self-esteem
by painting a brighter picture of a future self-image!
If you don't like today, be patient,
it's like the weather in Colorado, everyday is different.

I am consoling!

con*sol*ing *adj.* give solace or comfort; cheer up.

Be Constructive

Seek to improve the world around you
with your actions, opinions and comments.
You are responsible for building a future
that can stand up to your criticism.
Who are you kidding?
You know who you are and...
you can do anything you set your mind to.
Building blocks for Life and Light are all around:
look and see for yourself.

I am constructive!

con*struc*tive *adj.* 1. helping to improve: *constructive criticism.* 2. deduced by
inference or interpretation; inferential: *constructive permission.*

Be Cooperative

Be willing to work and act together today
for common purposes, in harmony.
Form groups of like-minded individuals
and move about like birds in a flock or fish in a school.
When in traffic, act and react as a team.
Move as one... within united states of mind!

I feel cooperative... I am cooperative!

co*op*er*a*tive *adj.* 1. working or acting together willingly for a common purpose
like getting from point *a* to point *b*. 2. demonstrating a willingness to cooperate.

Be Courageous

Be encouraged to know...
that the universe supports your success: your bliss.
Step forward into the uncertainty of days with certain knowledge
that you are never given anything that you can't handle.
Your brain is hardwired with the circuitry of courage
and with a simple flip of the switch
you can perform as you were designed to perform.
Flip that switch on... now! Command, "Yes! I can!"

I feel courageous... I am courageous!

cou*ra*ge*ous *adj.* 1. possessing the quality of mind or spirit that enables a
person to face difficulty, danger, pain, uncertainty, etc. 2. characterized by
courage; bravery or valiance. – *syn.* 1. fearlessness, dauntlessness, intrepidity,
fortitude, pluck, spirit. 2. COURAGE, BRAVERY, VALOUR, refer to qualities of
spirit and conduct. COURAGE permits a person to face extreme dangers and
difficulties without fear: *to take (or lose) courage.* BRAVERY implies true courage
together with daring and an intrepid boldness: *bravery in battle.* VALOUR implies
continuous active bravery in the face of personal danger, and a noble and lofty
quality of courage: *valor throughout a campaign; valor in fighting for the rights of
freedom and personal liberty.*

Be Courteous

When moving in traffic
or mingling with people in a crowded space
allow "common sense" to have a place in your considerations.
How you treat others
exhibits examples of how you wish to be treated.
Be considerate of others
when you're on a bus or in a theater or dinning room
and control your comm devices:
don't force others to listen in on your private affairs.

I feel courteous...

I am courteous.

cour*te*ous *adj.* having or showing good manners; polite.

Be Creative

Be original in your thinking and your expressions.
Be ingenious with imagination.
Tap into a pre-verbal frame of mind
and feel your way into notions, which have never been before.
Continue to ask, "What else is it?"
"How else can this be seen?"
"How else can this be done?"
"How else can this be shown?"

I feel creative... I am creative!

cre*a*tive *adj.* 1. having the quality or power of causing something to come into being, something unique that would not naturally evolve or that is not made by ordinary processes. 2. evolving from a person's own thought or imagination, as a work of art, an invention, etc.: *creative writing.* 3. producing an original product of mind especially an imaginative artistic work: *BeBe's ZenSwing.com® is a very creative effort.* 4. evolution: *the product went through many creative changes.*

Be Cultivating

Promote growth and development
of that which serves to bring happiness and success.
Plant each seed; provide water and sunshine for nourishment
then, stand back and watch the growth.
Protect your crops
from the predators of pessimism and other vicissitudes
while emotionally irrigating with plenty of patience.
Harvest the fruits of truth, beauty and goodness.
The rewards are fabulous attitudes with tasty moods of spirit.

I feel like cultivating...
I am cultivating!

cul*ti*vate *v.t.* 1. to prepare and work on (*land or mind*) in order to raise crops; till. 2. to use a cultivator on. 3. to promote or improve the growth of (*a plant, crop, etc.*) by labor and attention. 4. to produce by culture. 5. to develop or improve by education or training; refine. 6. to promote the growth or development of (*an art, science, etc.*); foster. 7. to devote oneself to (*an art, science, etc.*). 8. to seek to promote or foster (*friendship, love, etc.*) 9. to seek the arena of acquaintance or friendship of (*a person*).

Be Curious

Be inquisitive, desiring to learn and know.
And, as you wander through life, turn over many stones.
Then you won't reach the end of life
wondering what it was all about.
Intuition is a sensor
for things you should know but haven't yet confirmed.
Curiosity leads to knowledge:
peak your interest by learning all you can.

I am curious!

cu*ri*ous *adj.* 1. desirous of learning or knowing; inquisitive. 2. arousing interest or attention through being inexplicable or highly unusual; odd; strange: *a curious sort of person.*

51

Be Dancing

Let good feelings promote movement in your physical body.
Do a Snoopy Dog dance when feeling blissicity.
Move your body in joy
healing muscles, organs, brains and bones.
Put your hands in the air and let the light pour through you!
Come on now and shake your booty.
Shake your whammy fanny.

I feel like dancing....

I... am dancing.

danc*ing *adj.* moving one's feet, or body, or both, rhythmically in a pattern of steps, esp. to the accompaniment of music. 2. to leap, skip, jump, etc., as from excitement or emotion. 3. to bob up and down. (*Ed. Note.* A Snoopy Dog dance is credited to Charles Schulz, the creator of the Peanuts® Cartoon Series.)

Be Daring

Have the necessary courage to be and do something you desire.
Endorse feelings of faith in meeting your requirements
and have enough integrity to see endeavors through to fruition.
Take a chance on the unknown
and magnify the depth of your adventure in life.
Dive off the low diving board first
and then ascend to ever higher levels of attainment.

I feel daring...

I am daring!

dar*ing *n.* adventurous courage; boldness. – *adj.* bold; intrepid; adventurous. – *v.t.* to meet with defiantly.

Be Dauntless

Have a sense of purpose and fear nothing.
Boldness is kindred to genius.
Challenge others with positive urge
and promote affirmative principles.
Prefer qualities of substance to mudslinging campaigns of fear.

I feel dauntless...

I am dauntless!

daunt*less *adj.* 1. not to be overcome with fear; fearless. 2. intrepid; enheartened.
3. bold: *both he and she became dauntless moments before going on stage.*

Be Dear

You are loveable.
I love you.
You matter to me.
You are precious and 1st choice.
I bend over backwards for you.
I drive that extra mile... or two... for you.
You mean a lot to me.
Did I mention I love you?
I... love... you!

I feel dear...

I am dear.

dear *adj.* 1. beloved or loved. 2. precious in one's regard: *our dearest
possessions.* 3. heartfelt; earnest: *one dearest wish.*

Be Decisive

Engage powers of determination and display ability to choose.
Resolve personal willpower to pursue your goals and dreams.
Be free from ambiguity of what you want
and free from hesitation to receive it.
Many are called; few choose.
Command your mind to be made up.
"I make up my mind.
I've made up my mind"

I feel decisive...

I'm decisive!

de*ci*sive *adj.* 1. having the power or quality of deciding, as on a question or problem by making a judgment. 2. putting an end to controversy. 3. making up one's mind.

Be Delightful

Be responsible for the atmosphere you surround yourself with.
Afford pleasure and happiness
to those you love with laughter and cheer.
Let lightness of being permeate both thinking and feelings.
Spread feelings of infectious happiness.

I feel delightful...

I am delightful!

de*light*ful *adj.* 1. affording a high degree of pleasure or enjoyment; joy; rapture. 2. acting to give great pleasure. – *v.t.* . to have great pleasure; take pleasure (*followed by in or an infinitive*): *it's delightful when they're cooking fancy dishes.*

Be Desirable

Be excellent and worth desiring.
Be pleasing and fine for yourself first.
Dress yourself attractively.
Finish your posture with a smile.
Feature yourself to be the King or Queen
of the stories you tell yourself.
Feel delight in being the *Star of Your Show!*

I feel desirable...

I am desirable!

de*sir*able *adj.* 1. worth desiring; pleasing, excellent, or fine. 2. arousing desire or longing: *a desirable playmate.* 3. advisable; recommendable: *a desirable time.*

Be Determined

Leave this shore to find another.
Let go of this rung of the ladder for the next.
Be unwaveringly decided.
Persist in your choices.
Get good at moving through the terror barrier.
Be the commander of your Life and Light.
Go for it.

I feel determined...

I am determined!

de*ter*mined *adj.* 1. resolute; unfalteringly decided. 2. settled; resolved.

Be Different

Know that no one is identical
and enjoy feeling this distinction.
Separate yourself from others by degree of abstract quality.
Contrast is an ingredient of beauty
so, shine in this distinctive, commendable aura.
Being unique has the advantage of remembrance.

I feel different...

I am different!

dif*fer*ent *adj.* 1. differing in character or quality; not alike; dissimilar. 2. not identical; separate or distinct. 3. various; several.

Be Diligent

Be constant in your efforts to accomplish something.
Pursue your dreams, wishes and goals
with persevering attention.
Many little things add up to big things, so,
take each day as they come
by doing a little bit here and a little bit there.
You'll be amazed at how much can get done
with seemingly little effort.

I act diligent...

I am diligent!

dil*i*gent *adj.* 1. constant in effort to accomplish something. 2. done or pursued with persevering attention; painstaking: *a diligent search.*

Be Discerning

Mentally distinguish truth, beauty and goodness in your life.
Your faculty of intuition can assist with interpretation
of each thought, time, event and situation as they arrive.
There is only one mind, but with many connections:
become sensitive to your "feelers"; your scanners.
Learn to clean and monitor the filters you use to see through
and be a Van Guard for the values you adopt for yourself.

I feel discerning...

I am discerning!

dis*cern*ing *adj.* 1. showing good judgment and understanding. 2. perceiving
by sight, feeling, or some other sense. 3. cognizant of through the intellect.
4. recognize via mental faculties. (*Ed. Note.* Van Guard is the forefront of any
movement or adoption of attitude or modification of mind.)

Be Doing

Action (doing) is an integral part of being and having.
Performance and execution
are both important to manifesting desires.
Feel the necessary courage
and begin following through with each endeavor.
Use thought, wisdom and feelings
to empower accomplishments and achievements.

I am doing!

do*ing *v.* 1. taking action; performing. 2. making or preparing: *I'll be doing the
salad.* 3. create; form, or bring into being: *She's doing lovely oil portraits these
days.*

Be Dreaming

Indulge in your dreams and aspirations.
Lucidly imagine a bright future with many happy occasions.
Enhance each endeavor of your journey with visionary clarity
and fan the flame of your wishes into desires.
Build your castles in the sky
with your feet firmly planted on the ground of reality.

I am dreaming!

dream*ing *adj.* 1. voluntarily visioning while awake: *I'm dreaming of seeing you again.* 2. indulging in daydreams. 3. to think of, or conceive of, something in a very remote way. 4. to see or imagine in sleep or in a vision.

Be Dynamic

Explode with feelings of enthusiasm
and exude this essence with multiplicity in action.
Imbue self-esteem with exponential, effervescent emotion.
Move the magnet of your thoughts with feelings
and this power of your mind can move mountains.
Flex your muscles of eagerness with powerful intentions
and well-designed feeling programs for progress.

I feel dynamic...

I am dynamic!

dy*nam*ic *adj.* 1. pertaining to or characterized by energy or effective action.
2. vigorously active or forceful; energetic.

Be Easy

Let your disposition reflect attitudes of co-operation.
Get along with others and don't take things too seriously.
Adopt a mind-set, which reveals peace and good will.
Periodically enjoy uncomplicated and undemanding interludes.

I feel easy...

I am easy!

eas*y *adj.* 1. not difficult; requiring little effort or labor: *a book that is easy to read; an easy victory.* 2. free from pain, discomfort, worry or care: *an easy mind.* 3. providing, or conducive to, ease or comfort; comfortable: *an easy life.*

Be Ebullient

Find bliss within yourself.
Enjoy feeling tremendously elated and embrace this joy.
Feel extreme happiness bubble over
and spill out onto every cell within your body
to all those people surrounding you.
Amplify delight in manifesting destiny.
Catch your bliss and ride that puppy... all day long.

I feel ebullient...

I am ebullient!

e*bul*lient *adj.* 1. overflowing with fervor, enthusiasm, or excitement; high-spirited. 2. boiling up; bubbling up like a boiling liquid.

Be Eclectic

Select and use what you consider to be the best elements
of any system of medicine (care of the body),
philosophy (care of the mind),
or religion (care of the spirit.)
Perfection is a balancing act
of blending the most excellent of fruitful qualities.
Be unpredictable except in one area; be more positive.

I feel eclectic...

I am eclectic!

ec*lec*tic *adj.* 1. selecting; choosing from various sources. 2. made up of what is
selected from different sources. 3. not following any one system as of philosophy,
medicine, religion, etc., but selecting and using what are considered the best
elements of all systems.

Be Ecstatic

Let your emotions express rapturous delight
as all feels right or is becoming that way.
Quiver with excitement at the very thought of being "here!"
The rhapsody of life
awaits your passionate appreciation for enthusiasm.
Sing the "I'm In My Bliss!" song.
Make it up as you go!

I feel ecstatic... I am ecstatic!

ec*stat*ic *adj.* 1. of, or pertaining to, or characterized by, ecstasy. 2. subject to,
or in a state of, ecstasy; rapturous. 3. experiencing an overpowering emotion
or exaltation; a state of sudden, intense feeling. 4. enjoying rapturous delight.
5. whelmed by the frenzy of poetic inspiration. 6. mentally transported by
contemplation of divine things or ideals. (*Ed. Note.* Refer to the "*I'm In My Bliss
Song*" by BeBe at www.bebe.bz)

Be Educated

Receive instruction from the schooling available
by drawing upon your natural intelligence
and willingness to learn.
Let your teachers bring out the best in you.
Adopt attitudes that enhance being a student of Life and Light
and, if you really want to learn something, go teach it.
Publish the best of what you've learned.
Enjoy knowing that you know what you know
but also realize there is still much you don't know.
Remain ready to learn about the new world that yet exists.

I am educated!

ed*u*cat*ed *adj.* 1. having undergone education. 2. characterized by, or displaying qualities of, culture and learning. 3. based on some information or experience: *an educated estimate of sales.*

Be Effective

Whatever you set your mind to, produce the intended outcome.
The more you respond to something...
the more it stays... in your face.
When something works, repeat it,
if it doesn't work, try something else until it does work.
Results are the only fair way to gauge anyone or anything.
Burst forth with truly amazing and attractive results.

I feel effective...

I am effective!

ef*fec*tive *adj.* 1. adequate to accomplish a purpose; producing the intended or expected result: effective measures. 2. actually in operation or in force; functioning: *The law becomes effective at midnight.*

Be Elastic

Be capable of returning to your original self
after being stretched past your limits,
stressed by disappointment
and bent out of shape.
Have a springy mental and physical disposition.
When you're headed one-way and being pulled in another,
center your mind;
acquire an attitude for attending to both directions at once
in proper perspective.
Have courage.

I feel elastic...

I am elastic!

e*las*tic. *adj.* 1. capable of returning to its original length shape, etc. after being stretched, deformed, or expanded. 2. flexible; accommodating; tolerant: *an elastic conscience.* 3. springing back or rebounding; springy; resilient.

Be Elated

Happiness can never be over-rated.
You were designed to attain and maintain happiness
and remain so for most of each day and night.
Gratitude is the most powerful reason to feel happy.
Perceive the many reasons for feeling happy.
Let your insights provide stories of why you should be happy.

I feel elated...

I am elated.

e*lat*ed *adj.* very happy or proud; jubilant; in high spirits.

Be Eloquent

Exercise the power of fluent, forceful and appropriate speech.
Command yourself to speak your mind with clarity
at every reasonable opportunity.
Let off-the-cuff comments be predisposed
toward promoting the best of you and those around you.
Articulate and accentuate the finer points of Life and Light
and the relationships thereof.

I feel eloquent...

I am eloquent!

el*o*quent *adj.* 1. having or exercising the power of fluent, forceful, and
appropriate speech: *an eloquent orator.* 2. characterized by forceful and
appropriate expression: *an eloquent speech.* 3. movingly expressive: *looks
eloquent of admiration.*

Be Emancipated

Be released from bondage of fear
or anything that would constrict your free movement.
Be unhindered by custom, tradition, superstition or culture.
Move beyond indignity, betrayal and violation
and see these things as events, not as a status to be adopted.
Resume power to pursue personal liberty in life
and feel happiness in your ability to enjoy bliss.

I feel emancipated...

I am emancipated!

e*man*ci*pat*ed *adj.* 1. freed, as from slavery, bondage, or the like. 2. not
constrained or restricted by custom, tradition, superstition, etc.; uninhibited.
3. out of session or school for the summer or holidays.

Be Empathic

Be able to identify feelings, thoughts and attitudes of others.
Your ability to sense others' feelings can reveal many treasures.
As an empath... you can learn a great deal
by also listening to what's not spoken; seeing what's not visible.
Intuition guides you into understanding where others are.
Be able to read your audience.

I feel empathetic...

I am empathic!

em*path*ic *adj.* 1. intellectually identifying with or vicariously experiencing the
feelings, thoughts, or attitudes of another person. 2. imaginatively ascribing to an
object, as a natural object or work of art, feelings or attitudes present in oneself.

Be Enchanting

Find delight within yourself.
Keep focused on how you feel things can be
and instill these possibilities and insights in others by example.
Cast a spell... or, make a wish!
Paint peoples desires within your own.
The root word for magic
comes from the same root word for imagination.
Inspire others to believe in both magic and miracles.

I feel enchanting...

I am enchanting.

en*chant*ing *adj.* 1. charming; bewitching: *the young performer has an enchanting
effect on his audience.* 2. impart a magical quality or effect. 3. delighting to a high
degree; charm: *the preacher is quite enchanting.*

Be Encouraging

See beauty in others where they cannot see it for themselves.
Step up to the plate on their behalf and hit a home run.
Show by example how dreams are built and goals attained.
Be a role model and illustrate accomplishment
by demonstrating how good it feels to have courage.

I feel encouraging...

I am encouraging!

en*cour*ag*ing *adj.* 1. to inspire with courage, spirit, or confidence. 2. to stimulate by assistance, approval, etc.

Be Endless

Enlarge the insight of your involvement in existence.
Expand your perception of infinity and eternity.
Feel yourself move
within this never-ending age of Life and Light.
Slip into eternity
by acknowledging and embracing
this constant river of moments.

I feel endless...

I am endless!

end*less *adj.* without end.

Be Energetic

Flip your switch on and spark vivid, dynamic vitality
in your body, mind and spirit with youthful enthusiasm.
Overcome lethargy and laziness by freeing the child within you.
Reach out for fun, play and laughter.
Zip your do dah and zap your boo-day.
Get in touch with your energy.
Enjoy feeling it today.

I feel energetic...

I am energetic!

en*er*get*ic *adj.* 1 possessing or exhibiting energy; forcible; vigorous. 2. powerful in action or effect; effective.

Be Engaging

Have a winning smile and a pleasing influence on others.
Garner their attention with your wit and charming personality.
Remember however... leave your audience wanting more.
This attractive reputation will then precede you in the future.

I feel engaging...

I am engaging!

en*gag*ing *adj.* 1. winning; attractive; pleasing: *her engaging smile.* 2. attract and hold fast: *The Harry Potter novels are engaging pastimes for the childrens' attention and interest.*

Be Enlightened

Possess intellectual and spiritual insight
to the eternal here and now.
Be freed from ignorance and misinformation
by clearing the filters of your perception.
Open your mind and heart!
Allow the illumination of love and good will.
The mind is like a parachute, it only works when its open.
Let Life and Light be embossed upon the fabric of your soul.

I feel enlightened...

I am enlightened!

en*light*ened *adj.* given intellectual or spiritual light to; instruction; having been imparted knowledge to.

Be Enraptured

Be moved to rapture; delighted beyond measure,
and caught up in the rhapsody of your life.
Let the poetic charms of being alive captivate you.
Give permission for blissicity to re-energize your existence.
Be more than happy.

I feel enraptured...

I am enraptured!

en*rap*tured *adj.* 1. transported; entranced; enchanted. 2. fascinated; captivated; spellbound. 3. charmed; overjoyed; ecstatic. 4. delighted. (*Ed. Note*, blissicity is a combination word blending the words bliss and electricity: *a spiritual energy.*)

Be Enterprising

Find a need and fill it.
Acquire initiative, ingenuity and energy.
Necessity; the mother of invention enamors and embraces you.
Remember... you get to sleep in the bed you make,
so make sure its one you'll be happy with.
Create multiple streams of passive income.

I feel like being enterprising...

I am enterprising!

en*ter*pris*ing *adj.* 1. full of or characterized by great initiative, ingenuity, and energy. 2. maintaining dynamic boldness and cutting edge principia.

Be Entertaining

Know how to treat your guests.
Hold the attention of that which is agreeable
with that which is amusing.
Attend to details, which act to delight your company.
Provide both opening and closing acts for the main show.

I feel like entertaining...

I am entertaining!

en*ter*tain*ing *adj.* affording entertainment; amusing.

Be Enthusiastic

Breathe life into your experience
and watch your purposes explode.
Inspire your spirit to take a tour of happiness – beyond belief.
Allow your passion for Life and Light to animate your emotions.
Live unfettered and alive.

I feel enthusiastic...

I am enthusiastic!

en*thu*si*as*tic *adj.* full of or characterized by eagerness; excited; fervent.

Be Evolving

Unfold over time.
Become more of who you are
by blending your potentialities
into possibilities, into probabilities...
into actualities; a new creation.
Find spontaneity
within your personal library of character qualities.
Evolution "is" intelligent creation, intelligent design in action...
and, it's a good thing, a good thought, a good concept.

I... am evolving!

e*volv*ing *v.t.* 1. to develop gradually: *to evolve a scheme.* 2. to give off or emit,
an odors or vapors. – *v.i.* 1. to come forth gradually into being; develop; undergo
evolution: *the whole idea evolved from a casual remark.* 2. to change existence
into a new form: *She evolved into a dynamic president of the corporation.*

Be Excellent

Possess superior merit and feel remarkably good.
Be instilled with outstanding qualities and matchless integrity.
Excel at math, science, language and philosophy
or any career you choose.
And as above... so below, let your body match your mind:
participate in athletics.

I feel excellent...

I am excellent!

ex*cel*lent *adj.* possessing excellence or superior merit; transcend.

Be Exceptional

Be more than what you would be if you didn't care,
and more than what you would be if you didn't try.
Become what you feel and dream you can become.
Sparkle like the twinkle in your loved one's eye.

I feel exceptional...

I am exceptional!

ex*cep*tion*al *adj.* 1. forming an exception or unusual instance; rarely unusual.
2. extraordinary: *He was an exceptional example of a neighborhood leader.*

Be Exhilarating

Invigorate and stimulate pleasant, merry laughter,
with feelings of good cheer and enthusiasm.
Cause people to be more alive because of you.
Deliver results that make others more than glad they know you.
Walk into the room like you were walking onto your yacht.
"Where to... today... mon Capitan?"

I feel exhilarating...

I am exhilarating!

ex*hil*a*rat*ing *v.t.* 1. to enliven; invigorate; stimulate. 2. to make cheerful or merry.

Be Expedient

Do what it takes to get the job done... quickly,
without dragging your feet
and without destroying or injuring anyone in the process.
Do chores and homework right away
and be left with plenty of time for play.
Be methodical in your efforts
to anticipate and accomplish your goals and dreams.
These habits enable you to be extremely successful in life.

I am expedient!

ex*pe*di*ent. *adj.* 1. tending to promote some proposed or desired object; fit
or suitable under the circumstances. 2. conducive to advantage or interest of
happiness in the spirit of the law, as opposed to right or by the letter of the law.

Be Expressive

Enhance the effects of being heard
with appropriate gestures and manners.
Stand up straight
and let your posture convey feelings of confidence.
Let your hands, feet, eyes and eyebrows
move to provide emphasis.
Feel your thoughts come alive as you speak and write.

I feel expressive...

I am expressive!

ex*pres*sive *adj.* 1. serving to express; indicative of power to express: *a look expressive of gratitude.* 2. full of expression; meaningful: *an expressive shrug.*

 # Be Exquisite

Imagine the finest, most appealing thoughts you can
and revel in the presence of your regal nobility
all the while refining your tastes
to reflect the best in Life and Light.
You are truly on your way to being like your creator.

I feel exquisite...

I am exquisite.

ex*qui*site *adj.* 1. of special beauty or charm, or rare and appealing excellence, as a face, flower, scene of nature, etc. 2. extraordinarily fine; consummate: *exquisite weather.* 3. intense or keen as pleasure, feeling, etc. 4. keenly or delicately sensitive or responsive: an exquisite ear for music. 5. of rare excellence of production or workmanship.

Be Extraordinary

Be exceptional in character, and signify the remarkable.
Surprise yourself and others with how unique you can be.
Play Red Diamonds with yourself.
Stand out from the crowd.
Be you.

I feel extraordinary...

I am extraordinary!

ex*traor*di*nar*y *adj.* 1. beyond what is usual, ordinary, or established: *extraordinary powers of the President; extraordinary costs.* 2. exceptional in character, degree, etc.; noteworthy; remarkable: *extraordinary beauty.* (*Ed. Note.* Red Diamonds is a game where the participant contrives a symbol or signal to receive from the universe to show that the universe is listening to the participant, i.e. *She chose red diamonds to be the signal from the universe that her prayers were being heard. Red diamonds were soon seen, everywhere.*)

Be Fabulous

Feel exceptionally good and unusual.
Familiarize yourself with being marvelous,
and recognize magnificent occurrences as they take place.
Blossom into the incredible person you know you are.
Claim your right to be spectacular
and see yourself as awe-inspiring.
Be what legends are made of.

I feel fabulous... I am fabulous!

fab*u*lous *adj.* 1. almost unbelievable; incredible. 2. exceptionally good or unusual; marvelous; superb. 3. told or known though fables, myths, or legends.

Be Fair

Play the game of life as "I Win - You Win."
Discover what it's like
to feel free from bias, dishonesty and injustice.
Often harsh,
the only fair way to gauge anyone or anything is by results,
so, think before you act
because your actions have consequences beyond belief.
"Would you rather be happy or right?"
Being fair of face reflects beauty beyond the marrow
in a place no scientist can observe.

I feel fair...

I am fair!

fair *adj.* 1. legitimately sought, pursued, done, given, etc.; proper under the rules: *a fair fight.* 2. moderately large; ample: *a fair income.* 3. marked by favoring conditions; likely; promising: *in a fair way to succeed.* 4. pleasing in appearance; attractive: *a fair young maiden.* 5. courteous. 6. clear; easy to read.

Be Faithful

Faith is the act of supporting someone or something
for no reason or justification at all.
Let imagination sustain your faith.
Be impeccable with your words and keep your promises.
Be reliable in teamwork, trustworthy in confidence
and believable as witness.
Experience feelings of deep satisfaction in allegiance to truth.
Exhibit loyalty and belief in others as well as in yourself.

It feels good... to feel faithful...
I am faithful!

faith*ful *adj.* 1. true to one's word, promises, vows, etc. 2. steady in allegiance of affection. 3. adhering, or true to fact or an original: *a faithful account; a faithful copy.*

Be Fearless

Beckon that which is bold and brave within you.
Reckon with that which you fear.
Draw from the part of you that knows no fear.
Its been said that F.E.A.R. is False Evidence Appearing Real.
Abolish fear by seeing it as funny and yelling, "Ridiculous!" at it.
Be the champion.

I am fearless!

fear*less *adj.* 1. free from any distressing emotions aroused by an impending pain, danger, evil, etc., or by the illusion of such. 2. intrepid, dauntless: *fearless in the face of uncertainty.*

Be Feeling

Embrace each gut sensation (hunch) you have
as a signal from your intuition for quick perception.
Become acquainted with this "beyond-thinking" part of yourself.
Give yourself permission
for a capacity of emotions, especially for compassion.
Remember, all the time and money in the world
is spent on feeling... so, make sure you spend yours
on what feels good, promotes truth and is truly beautiful.

I am feeling!

feel*ing *v.i.* consciously perceiving a state of mind or a condition of body: *to be feeling happy; feeling well.* – *adj.* 1. sensitive; sentient. 2. readily affected by emotion; empathetic: *a feeling heart.*

Be Festive

When it's time to party... party hearty.
Laugh and contribute to the joy of celebration.
Let your feeling of merriment encourage peers to participate.
Dance and be happy.

I feel festive...

I am festive!

fes*tive *adj.* 1. pertaining to or suitable for a feast or festival: *festive decorations; a festive meal.* 2. joyous; merry.

Be Flexible

Life is in constant motion.
Be pliable enough to meet any challenges
and willing to yield, being so strong that you can put others first.
Would you rather be right or happy?
Failures and disappointments are simply an event, not a status.
Be capable of being bent without breaking.

I feel flexible...

I am flexible!

flex*i*ble *adj.* 1. susceptible to modification or adaptation; adaptable: *a flexible schedule.* 2. willing or disposed to yield; pliable: *a flexible personality.*

Be Focused

Adjust whatever's necessary
to become clearer and more sharply defined.
Your thinking, seeing, feeling, speaking and general well-being
deserve to be commanded with clarity.
Concentrate on observing thoughts and things
in the spirit intended.
Only you have the privilege of seeing through your eyes.

I am focused!

fo*cused *adj.* 1. the clear and sharply defined condition of an image. 2. a central
point of attraction, attention, or activity. 3. to concentrate: *to focus one's thoughts.*

Be Forgiving

"Be ye perfect, even as I am."
If this were a perfect universe,
that statement would never have been made.
There is much room for improvement
and infinite space for making mistakes.
Allow your nature to include,
mercy and compassion, tolerance and forgiveness,
for yourself... as well as others.

I am forgiving.

I am forgiven.

for*giv*ing *adj.* 1. to grant free pardon for or remission of *(an offense, debt, etc.)*;
absolve. 2. to give up all claim on account of; remit (*a debt, obligation, etc.*)
3. to grant free pardon to a person, place, thought or thing. 4. to cease to feel
resentment against: *I'm forgiving you for being late.*

Be Free

You cannot enjoy free will without freedom recognized.
Move through life with a sense of elbowroom.
Promote thoughts or things,
that endorse potential, possible perspectives.
Shadows fall into place in the presence of light.
Take pleasure in your personal rights and liberty,
and respect the same for others.

I feel free... I... am free!

free *adj.* 1. enjoying political independence: *free from political hound-dogs.*
2. existing under, characterized by, or possessing civil, political, or religious
liberties. 3. able to do something at will; at liberty. 4. acting with self-restraint and
reserve. 5. able to enter, move and enjoy at will: *feel free to move about the cabin.*

Be Friendly

In order to have friends, be one.
Invite others to make friends with you.
Send or leave notes of cheer and goodwill
and let people know you're thinking well of them.
Invite companions to participate in this,
your Odyssey of Life,
by sharing
significant feelings, experiences, observations and insights.
And, listen to your friends, if you want them to listen to you.

I feel friendly...

I am friendly!

friend*ly *adj.* 1. characteristic of or befitting a friend. 2. like a friend; kind; helpful.
3. favorably disposed; inclined to approve, help, or support. 4. not hostile or at
variance; amicable: *friendly neighborhood.* 5. someone to hang out with; doing
stuff together; sharing hobbies and interests: *You are a friendly part of my life!*

Be Fulfilled

Refine your ability to appreciate feeling satisfied.
Notice beauty and value in small things, as well as large.
Embrace the people in your life with love
and hold dear your achievements.
Find and share satisfaction with others verbally and non-verbally
at the same time it occurs.

I feel fulfilled...

I am fulfilled!

ful*filled *v.t.* 1. to carry out, or bring to realization, as a prophecy, promise, etc.
2. to perform or do, as duty; obey or follow, as commands. 3. to satisfy
(*requirements, obligations, etc.*) 4. to bring to an end; finish or complete, as a
period of time. 5. to develop the full potential of. 6. matured; ripe.

Be Fun

Provide enjoyment and happiness at work and play.
Seek delight when you're with your friends as well as by yourself.
Nourish your spirit with a sense of true pleasure.
Frolic in the high spirits of freedom.

I feel fun...

I am fun!

fun *adj.* 1. of, or pertaining to, fun, especially to social fun. 2. whimsical;
flamboyant: *the fashions she wears are definitely on the fun side.*

Be Gallant

For both men and women,
be elegant with your politeness and attention.
Free your high-spirited nature to exist.
Rise to the challenge of being noble.
Be the trend that sets the fashion.

I am gallant!

gal*lant *adj.* 1. brave, high-spirited, or chivalrous: *a gallant knight.* 2. stately; grand;
elegant. 3. polite and attentive to others; courtly. 4. amorous; amatory.

Be Generous

Be free from meanness or smallness of mind or character.
Be liberal in the giving
of your time, talents, treasures and energy.
Be an angel for others and observe angels show up for you.
And give, as you have been given to.

I feel generous...

I am generous!

gen*er*ous *adj.* 1. liberal in giving; munificent; unselfish, 2. large; abundant;
ample. 3. rich or strong in flavor: a generous wine.

Be Gentle

Be kind and amiable.
Base your life upon that, which is mild,
carefully sensitive, soft and loving.
Ingeniously transform fighting into friendship.

I feel I'm gentle...

I... am gentle.

gen*tle *adj.* 1. kindly or amiable. 2. mild; not harsh, coarse, or vicious; moderate.
3. gradual: *a gentle slope.* 4. easily managed; tractable. 5. polite; refined.

Be Genuine

Embrace the authentic.
Feel how enlightening it is to not have to pretend...
to just be yourself.
Be free from any pretense and deceit
by remembering just how unique you are.
Proceed as from the original stock,
the original thought, the original feeling.

I feel genuine...

I am genuine!

gen*u*ine, *adj.* 1. possessing the purported character, quality, or origin; authentic.
2. properly so called: *a genuine case of smallpox.* 3. free from pretense,
affectation, or hypocrisy; sincere. 4. pure in breed: *the Black Russian terrier is a
genuine working breed of dog.*

Be Glad

Attend your presence with all things positive.
Find courage in your feelings of bliss
and be pleased in your observations of joy.
Seek the light of happiness to dissolve shadows of sadness.
Appreciate thankfulness in gratitude.

I feel glad...

I am glad!

glad *adj.* 1. feeling joy or pleasure; delighted; pleased. 2. attended with or causing joy or pleasure: *a glad occasion.* 3. characterized by or showing cheerfulness, joy, or pleasure, as looks, utterances, presence, etc.

Be Glowing

Display radiance of health,
and let the rich colors of life emanate from your skin.
Let the sparkle of your mind twinkle in your eyes,
and permit the fullness of heart-felt thanks
to be radiant through your smile.
Experience what it's like to be "more than happy."

I feel I'm glowing...

I am glowing!

glow*ing *adj.* 1. incandescent. 2. rich and warm in coloring: *glowing colors.* 3. showing the radiance of health, excitement, etc. 4. warmly favorable or complimentary: *a glowing account of his valor.*

Be Gracious

Characterize your personality with qualities of good taste.
Move yourself in a world-class manner.
Openly show tolerance to those around you.
Apply courtesy and compassion
to the gestures you make towards others.
Exercise your talent for being pleasingly acceptable
and elegantly detailed.
Honor will-dignity in life and poise yourself for appreciation
by promoting gratitude for Life and Light.

I feel gracious... I am gracious!

gra*cious. *adj.* 1. disposed to show grace or favor; kind; benevolent; courteous.
2. characterized by good taste, comfort, ease, or luxury: gracious suburban
living. 3. indulgent or beneficent in a pleasantly condescending way, especially to
inferiors. 4. merciful or compassionate. 5. fortunate or happy.

Be Grateful

Gratitude is the first step in appreciation.
Desire to expand your capacity for feeling positive reception.
Experience first hand what its like
to receive the wishes you've turned into desires.
Demand feelings of thankfulness and appreciation
to spark excitement in your emotional experience.

I am grateful.

I feel grateful.

grate*ful adj.1. warmly or deeply appreciative of kindness or benefits received;
thankful: *I am grateful to you for your kindness.* 2. expressing or actuated by
gratitude: *a grateful letter from grateful contemplation.* 3. pleasing to the mind or
senses; agreeable or welcome; refreshing: *the grateful sound of rain.*

Be Great

Be of high principle and enroll others to do likewise.
Gloom cannot exist in the observance of happiness felt.
Stand steadfast when believing in positive values
and cultivate optimistic meanings throughout life.
The quality of your reputation
will be remembered... long after you've gone.

I feel great...

I am great!

great *adj.* 1. unusually or comparatively large in size or dimensions; big. 2. large in number; numerous. 3. unusual or considerable in degree, power, intensity, etc.: *great pain.* 4. notable; remarkable; exceptionally outstanding: *a great occasion.* 5. distinguished; famous: *a great inventor.* 6. important; highly significant or consequential: *a great era in history.* 7. being such in extreme degree: *great friends.* 8. of extraordinary powers; having unusual merit; very admirable: *a great statesman or stateswoman.*

Be Gregarious

Mishmosh at art shows and mingle at dinners.
Hang out with friends and chitchat with family.
Enjoy meeting new people and develop a vital, viral social web.
Allow yourself to enjoy the company of loved ones
as well as those you've just met.

I feel gregarious...

I am gregarious!

gre*gar*i*ous *adj.* 1 fond of the company of others; sociable. 2. living or traveling in flocks or herds, as animals: *My gregarious nature was released at the zoo this past weekend.*

Be Happy

Contemplate thoughts that are delightful
and feelings that are pleasing.
Be apt for joy
and felicitous through your actions, utterances and ideas.
Enjoy a rich inner life
with your considerations, viewpoints and sense of humor.
Have a propensity to laugh, creating relief for those around you.

I feel happy... I am happy!

hap*py *adj.* 1. delighted, pleased, or glad, as over any particular thing.
2. characterized by or indicative of pleasure, contentment, or joy: *a happy mood.*
3. favored by fortune; fortunate or lucky: *a happy occurrence.*

Be Harmonious

Sing your melody...
because your melody
can sound like harmony to someone else's melody.
Help form a pleasingly consistent wholeness within and without.
Pick up the slack
whenever you observe how you can assist others.
Be congruent and agreeable
in your thoughts, feelings and actions,
creating euphony within and about you.
Superimpose body, mind and spirit in alignment with each other
in order to utilize the magnetic energy of blissicity.

I feel harmonious... I am harmonious!

har*mo*ni*ous. *adj.* 1. marked by agreement in feeling or action: *a harmonious group.* 2. forming a pleasingly consistent wholeness; congruous: *harmonious colors.* 3. agreeable to the ear; tuneful; melodious. (*Ed. Note.* – blissicity is a combination word of bliss and electricity. It describes spiritual energy you can feel. *To feel it for yourself ... focus on a good feeling within you and allow it to snowball, ever larger until every cell in your body is pulsing with happiness.*)

Be Healthy

Be in a constant state of healing.
Every day you replace millions of cells and
every seven years you've replaced your entire body.
Learn to nourish your body, mind and spirit
in order to maintain a state of health that's free of dis-ease.

I am healthy.

I feel healthy. Yay!

health*y *adj.* 1. possessing or enjoying good health or a sound and vigorous mentality. 2. pertaining to, or characteristic of good health, or a sound and vigorous mind.: *a healthy appearance, healthy attitudes.* 3, conducive to health; healthful: *healthy recreation.*

Be Helpful

Be of service and quick to give assistance.
Act as an extra set of eyes, hands or feet for others.
In helping someone else... you help yourself: think about it.
Angel energy lubricates society.
Participate!

I am helpful!

help*ful *adj.* giving or rendering aid or assistance, of service.

Be Heroic

Act as a role model for others.
A "future you" endeavors to spark your imagination.
Take the insight of your ideals and adopt them for yourself.
Modify your thinking
to include observing and performing feats of greatness
and other magical acts of kindness.

I feel heroic...

I am heroic!

he*ro*ic *adj.* 1. of, pertaining to, or characteristic of, a person distinguished by courage or ability, admired for their brave deeds and noble qualities. 2. suitable to the character of a hero in size or concept; daring; noble: *a heroic ambition.* 3. having or displaying the character or attributes of someone considered a rolemodel or an ideal; extraordinarily bold, altruistic, determined, etc.: *He is a heroic explorer.* 4. dealing with or describing the deeds, attributes of heroes, as in literature: *She was not only beautiful, but heroic as well.*

Be Hip

Keep your eyes and ears open for the leading edge of fashion.
Be aware of the latest trends,
styles of clothing and topics of conversation.
Know what the latest techniques
for touch and technologies afford.
Feel... on the leading edge of your attention span.
And... as you so desire... "Your Wish is my Command!"

I feel hip...

I am hip.

hip *adj.* familiar with the latest ideas, styles, etc. informed; knowledgeable.

Be Home

Make yourself at home.
Feel comfortable in finding glasses for drinks of water.
Welcome home from 'cross the lands
now go straight in and wash your hands and remember,
return the lid to its down position... its a sign of being civilized.
Feel at ease in expressing delight in conversations
and happiness in pleasure received.
Others will inform you if any boundaries have been stepped over.

I feel at home... I am home.

home *adj.* 1. in one's own grounds or place of residence. 2. prepared to receive
guests. 3. in a situation familiar to one; at ease. 4. well-informed; proficient.
5. deep; to the heart; effectively and completely: *They made themselves at home.*

Be Honest

See clearly and speak the truth!
Show fairness and sincerity.
Feel genuine and unadulterated.
Signify the admirable in principles, intentions and actions.
Were you to steal from others...
you would be stealing from yourself:
that's not smart.
When lying to others...
you learn to lie to yourself: that's dangerous for you.
When learning how to believe, do so within yourself to yourself.
You are honorable only when you are honest.

I feel honest... I am honest!

hon*est *adj.* 1. honorable in principles, intentions, and actions; upright. 2. showing
uprightness and fairness: *honest dealings.* 3. gained fairly: honest wealth.
4. sincere; frank: *an honest face.* 5. genuine or unadulterated: *honest weight.*
6. respectable; having a good reputation: *an honest name.* 7. truthful or creditable:
an honest reputation; an honest resume.

Be Hopeful

Hope is the lifeblood of success,
a close relative of faith, stimulator of the imagination.
When learning how to believe,
hope becomes the application of your attitudes.
It is the act of believing in, but having not yet seen,
where certainty of conviction rules.
Promote probabilities with your mind
by coming up with ideas
for infinite potentialities and possibilities.

I feel hopeful... I am hopeful!

hope*ful *adj.* 1. full of hope; expressing hope: *hopeful words.* 2. exciting hope; promising advantage or success: *a hopeful prospect.*

Be Hospitable

Receive and treat guests and strangers
as you feel you would want to be treated;
warmly and generously.
Learn how to expect the unexpected
in order to make the most of life.
A stranger is only someone whose name you don't know yet.
Guided by intuition, provide people with the benefit of the doubt
until proven differently or as based upon previous experience.

I feel hospitable...

I am hospitable!

hos*pi*ta*ble *adj.* 1. receiving or treating guests or strangers warmly and generously: *a hospitable family.* 2. characterized by, or betokening, warmth and generosity toward guests or strangers: *a hospitable smile.* 3. favorably open (*usually followed by to*): *to be hospitable to new ideas.*

Be Humble

Allow neither praise nor slander to influence you.
Know who you feel you are
but let others discover it for themselves.
Be acquainted with whereof you speak,
or keep your mouth shut.
It's always better to keep others guessing;
not proving them right or wrong.
Humility requires you to observe without judgment.
Acknowledge mistakes, realize limits and respect others.
Learn to toot your horn without bragging.

I feel humble...

I am humble!

hum*ble *adj.* 1. not proud or arrogant, modest. 2. unpretentious.

Be Humorous

Do not take yourself so seriously that you cannot appreciate
the music of laughter and feelings of happiness.
There are so many layers and levels of situations and memories
that can be made light of and found to be truly funny.
Remember; find ways to laugh "with" those around you,
not "at" them.
Feel a hopeful sense of humor pervading Life and Light.
Humor acts as an antidote
for taking yourself and life too seriously.

I feel humorous...

I am humorous!

hu*mor*ous *adj.* 1. characterized by humor; funny; comic: *the humorous side of life.* 2. having or showing a sense of humor. 3. causmic humor; cosmic humor.

Be Idealistic

Pursue those concepts and things,
which you believe, ought to be.
Seek inner peace and stability
to promote insight into the ideal life.
Shoot for the moon and aim for the stars
when plotting your escape into liberty and beyond.
The world is rich with ideas; now fill it with ideals that match.
Picture yourself being noble and grand.
See yourself as truly blessed and note-worthy.

I am idealistic!

i*de*al*is*tic *adj.* 1. of, or pertaining to, idealism or idealists. 2. cherishing
or pursuing high or noble principles, purposes, goals, etc. 3. making ideal;
representing in an ideal form or character; exalted to an ideal perfection of
excellence. 4. striving toward something worthy of being imitated. 5. conducting
and achieving that which is considered worthy of being followed and modeled
after. 6. worshipful.

Be Imaginative

Foster your creativity and exploit your imagination.
Investigate ways to free your thoughts and your thinking.
Visualize something not actually present in the "real" world.
Enjoy as much sight, sound, texture, taste,
and feeling as you can call forth.
Use your minds' eye to observe things
beyond the scope of physical appearance and perception.

I am imaginative!

im*ag*i*na*tive *adj.* 1. characterized by, or bearing evidence of, imagination.
2. of, pertaining to, or concerned with the faculty of producing ideal creations
consistent with reality: *truly imaginative decor.* 3. having exceptional powers of
meeting with and resolving difficulties; resourceful: *imaginative solutions.*
4. the faculty of creating a series of images which depict concepts, dialog scripts,
scenery, and vicarious personalities.

Be Improvising

Be spontaneous in living your life every day.
Act whimsically, even without previous preparation.
Trust the ancient wisdom
within your identity, instincts and insights.
Sharpen creative edges through the décor of mind and home.
Apply on-the-spot thinking and quick perception.

I feel like improvising...

I am improvising!

im*pro*vis*ing *v.t.* 1. to perform or provide without previous preparation;
extemporize. 2. to compose (*verse, music, etc.*) on the spur of the moment. 3. to
recite, sing, etc. upon a moments notice: *called upon without warning, she had to
be improvising everything.*

Be In Love

Find yourself attracted to and in love with another person
based on what they represent for you,
and what they mean to you.
Appropriately express invitations for togetherness
and appreciate each other's presence.
Share your dreams and learn more about each other daily.
Be Love... falling in Love... with Love.

I feel I'm in love

I am... in love.

in love *adj.* feeling deep affection or passion for (*a person, idea, occupation, etc.*);
enamored of: *in love with life; in love with one's work; in love with you!*

Be Incomparable

Refrain from contrasting yourself with others.
Your harshest critic will always be yourself.
The measure of all things is relative,
so, possess your own set of standards.
You've never been before.
You are becoming more you each day.
You are unique and fantastic.
Embrace that embraceable you!

I... am incomparable!

in*com*pa*ra*ble *adj.* 1. matchless or unequaled: incomparable beauty.
2. not validly comparable, as two or more unlike objects; incommensurable.

Be Incredible

Inspire others with your life.
Adopt all the attitudes showcased in this book,
and discover for yourself
the effects of mentally devouring these Fruits of the Spirit.
Define your own path of Life and Light
and do what you dream of doing.
Be indescribably good
and personally yummy in oh so many ways.

I feel incredible...

I am incredible!

in*cred*i*ble *adj.* 1. so extraordinary as to not seem possible: *incredible speed.*
2. not credible; unbelievable: *the plot of the book is incredible.* 3. beyond belief.

Be Independent

Establish life, happiness and the pursuit of liberty for yourself.
Rely on your own abilities and resources.
Stand up for your rights and declare your responsibilities.
Empower your independence
by cultivating your presence of mind.

I am independent!

in*de*pend*ent *adj.* 1. not influenced or controlled by others in matters of opinion, conduct, etc. 2. not subject to another's authority or jurisdiction. 3. not guided by others: *independent research.* 4. not depending or contingent upon something else for existence, operation, etc. 5. not relying on another or others for aid or support. 6. possessing sufficient financial resources to be free of another's control or the need to work. 7. free from party or bipartisan commitments in politics.

Be Ingenious

Take the light of intelligence and bend it.
Look at thoughts, things and feelings in ways no one else does.
Ask yourself, "I see what that looks like, but... what else is it?"
Apply clever solutions and resourceful approaches
and make yourself a valuable associate.

I'm ingenious!

in*gen*ious *adj.* 1. characterized by cleverness or originality of invention or construction. 2. cleverly inventive; resourceful in contriving new explanations or methods and the like: *an ingenious executive.*

Be Inquisitive

Knowledge is asking and finding.
Experience is involvement and refinement.
The curious look within the vaults of the unknown
and make fresh ancient ideals.
Wisdom focuses free will for exploration and discovery.
Inquire within for answers without and about.
Answers satisfy the soul
and saturate the mind with inspiration.

I feel inquisitive...

I am inquisitive!

in*quis*i* tive. *adj.* 1. given to inquiry or research; eager for knowledge; curious: *an inquisitive mind.* 2. unduly curious; prying.

Be Inspired

Take a deep breath through your nose...
Now blow out hard... slowly through pursed lips.
Let this respiration instill enough oxygen for you to enjoy bliss.
Simply enough, the brain operates on oxygen and glucose.
Glucose is the "sugar" fuel; oxygen ignites that fuel.
Your brain needs both to become enlightened.
Wishes on fire turn into desire.

I feel inspired...

I am inspired.

in*spired *adj.* 1. aroused, animated, or imbued with the spirit to do a certain thing, by or as by supernatural or divine influence: *an inspired poet.* 2. resulting from such inspiration: *an inspired poem.* 3. inhaled: *inspired air.*

Be Interested

Participate in activities,
which have the power to engage your curiosity.
Display attentiveness
for what peaks the interests of your desires.
Invest considerations and feelings toward goals of your estate.
Cultivate your observation and participation in life.

I feel interested...

I am interested!

in*ter*est*ed *adj.* 1. having an interest in something; concerned: *interested members will meet at two.* 2. participating; having an interest or share; having money involved. 3. having the attention or curiosity engaged: *an interested spectator.*

Be Intentional

By right of free will... intention... do you create your world?
Feel unfettered and alive with genuine feelings for living life.
Place care in how you craft yourself
with possibilities, potentialities and probabilities.
Take command of your thinking, feeling, and language
and do things on purpose.
It's just as easy to imagine 5 million dollars,
as it is to imagine 5 dollars.

I feel intentional...

I am intentional.

in*ten*tion*al *adj.* 1. done deliberately or on purpose: an intentional remark.
2. of or pertaining to intention or purpose. 3. *Philosophy. a.* pertaining to
an appearance, phenomenon, or representation in the mind; phenomenal;
representational. *b.* pertaining to the capacity of the mind to refer to an existent or
nonexistent object. *c.* pointing beyond itself, as consciousness, a sign, etc.

Be Intuitive

Have gut feelings
and follow unconfirmed belief in things that matter.
Trust each step
brings you closer to your dreams, goals and desires.
Intuition is a peripheral feeling...
its about what's right in front of you
or heading your way.
Instinct guides you toward the next step
like truth ringing the bell of liberty.
Listen to your heart and trust your (gut) feelings.

I feel intuitive... I am intuitive.

in*tu*i*tive *adj.* 1. perceiving by a direct perception of truth, fact, etc. independent of any reasoning process: *immediate apprehension.* 2. perceived by resulting from or involving intuition: *intuitive knowledge.* 3. having or possessing intuition: *an intuitive person.*

Be Inventive

Create new products, ideas and techniques
by envisioning better methods, ideals and ways of doing things.
Act on your instincts to improve conditions,
and have a propensity to be inspired by others, or from within.
Necessity may well indeed be the mother of invention
but the thrill of innovation is her lover.
Open the window of your mind and feel refreshing winds of life
breathing in a wealth of discoveries and treasures.
Let the rubber of your soles hit the road; pursue your dreams.

I am inventive!

in*ven*tive *adj.* 1. apt at inventing, devising, or contriving. 2. having the function of inventing. 3. pertaining to, involving, or showing new, useful processes or machine improvement that did not exist previously and that is not obvious to persons artfully skilled in that field.

Be Inviting

Offer friendship, which is both attractive and alluring.
Request the presence and participation
of family, friends and associates
with a kind, courteous, and complementary atmosphere.
Send invitations to others so they may plan to attend your events.
Maps, times, and pertinent details result in successful soirees.

I am inviting!

in*vit*ing *adj.* offering an invitation, especially one of an attractive or tempting nature: *an inviting offer to join.*

Be Involved

Engage your interests
by adding emotion to the intentions and purposes you adopt.
Get into the thick of it and contribute your ideas with effort.
Participate personally in life including those you love
with consideration of the lives of others.
You matter, and so do they.

I feel involved...

I am involved!

in*volved *adj.* 1. to combine inextricably. 2. to bring into, an intricate form of, condition. 3. to engage the interests of emotions or commitment of.

Be Jazzed

Choose to be alive and spirited.
Approach life with an inclination for the offbeat
and emulate the privilege to improvise.
Take the best outlook, the most tasteful styles
and the most positive energy of your generation
and claim it as your own.
Anchor the zeal for your meal to the beat of your feet
and tap your toes in time.

I feel jazzed...

I am jazzed!

jazzed *adj.* 1. lively or spirited. 2. to put vigor or liveliness into *(usually followed by up)*: *I'm so jazzed up to go this weekend!*

Be Jovial

Being happy brings forth the benefits of health and prosperity.
Bliss is the way to say "thank you"
to the universe for answering your "want ads."
Being jovial allows others space for time
and time for space in being happy, too.
Life, is a cornucopia of good feelings... about feeling good.

I am jovial.

I feel jovial.

jo*vi*al *adj.* 1. endowed with or characterized by a hearty, joyous humor or a spirit of good fellowship. 2. of or pertaining to Jove or Jupiter and supposed to exert a happy influence.

Be Joyful

Feel full of glee in expressing thrill for life.
Spread happiness and be of good cheer.
Whistle to your hearts delight and hum a cheery tune.
You're dreaming up something
and everyone else wants to know what it might be.

I feel joyful...

I am joyful!

joy*ful *adj.* 1. full of joy, as a person, the heart, etc.; glad; delighted. 2. showing or expressing joy, as looks, actions, speech, etc,: *joyful sounds emanated from within.* 3. causing or bringing joy, as an event, a sight, news, etc.; delightful.

Be Judgeless

Avoid forming inflexible judgments and unalterable estimations.
Promote creativity; don't cultivate pigeon-holed beliefs.
Go past limits; they're just an event, not a status.
Suspend closure of mind... for as long as possible.
You can only see the road you're on... up to a certain point!
Who can say what's beyond the bend.

I remain judgeless!

judge*less *adj.* 1. beyond reproach. 2. self-governed. 3. inestimable.

Be Judicious

Exercise your faculty of good judgment.
Choose to be wise, sensible and well advised.
It's in your nature to have free will.
So exercise balance in judgements daily,
and... when in doubt, apply love.

I feel like being judicious...

I am judicious!

ju*di*cious *adj.* 1. using or showing judgment as to action or practical expediency; discreet, prudent, or politic. 2. having, exercising, or characterized by good judgment; wise, sensible, or well-advised.

Be Keen

Be highly sensitive and sharply perceptive.
Be enthusiastic in your endeavors and ardent in your dreams.
Live on the cutting edge of technology
and in touch with the leading edge of touch.
Get out there before anyone else
and claim your seat in the audience of Life and Light.

I feel keen...

I am keen!

keen *adj.* 1. finely sharpened, so as to cut or pierce readily: a keen knife. 2. sharp, piercing, or biting: *a keen wind; keen satire.* 3. highly sensitive or perceptive: *keen hearing; keen mind.*

Be Kind

Preoccupy yourself with loving dispositions.
Identify with those of like heart, similar feelings
and copacetic thinking.
Promote angel energy by being an angel for others
so angels show up for you.
Choose to be gracious and giving.

I feel kind... I am kind!

kind *adj.* 1. of a good or benevolent nature or disposition, as a person: *a kind guardian.* 2. having, showing, or proceeding from benevolence: *kind words.* – *syn.* KIND, GRACIOUS, KINDHEARTED imply a sympathetic attitude toward others, and a willingness to do good or give pleasure. KIND implies a deep-seated characteristic shown either habitually or on occasion by considerate behavior: *a kind father.* GRACIOUS often refers to kindness from a superior or older person to a coordinate, an inferior, a child, etc.: *a gracious monarch.* KINDHEARTED implies an emotionally sympathetic nature, sometimes easily imposed upon: *a kindhearted old woman.*

Be Kissable

Be genuine and modify yourself only toward the positive.
Maintain a timely condition
of having an air of being touchable, cute and cuddly.
In the story you tell yourself about you...
choose to be a character
which is physically, mentally and spiritually
attractive, beautiful and yummy.
Promote textures and qualities in yourself
that are to be admired, beheld and adored.

I feel kissable... I am kissable.

kiss*a*ble *adj.* inspiring the desire to kiss through being physically attractive: *I put my cute on and now I feel so... kissable. :)*

Be Knowing

Much is expected from those who know much.
Embrace that, which you're familiar with
and enjoy the insight of this awareness.
Give yourself credit for all your experiences.
Let ancient wisdom guide your intuition.

I am knowing!

know*ing *adj.* 1. shrewd, sharp, or astute. 2. affecting or suggesting shared knowledge of secret or private information: *a knowing glance.* 3. having knowledge or information; intelligent; wise. 4. conscious; intentional; deliberate.

Be Leading

Be a leader even with no one following you.
Be able to lead your self.
Learn to be a great follower and you create a great leader.
Choose positive causes and reasons
for the choices you choose to expect;
from the desires you project...
as you throw your dreams upstream
from the Bridge over Wishing River.
Guide your thinking with storyboards
and control your actions through planning.
Design majestic tones,
by enrolling attractive moods from the actors...
on the stage of your life.

I am leading!

lead*ing *v.t.* 1. to take the lead or conduct the way; go before or with to show the way: *leading a group on a cross-country hike.* 2. to conduct by holding and guiding: *leading a horse by a rope.* 3. to guide in direction, course, action, opinion, etc.; taking. 4. to go at the head of or in advance of (*a procession, list, body, etc.*); proceed first in. 5. acting as a leader.

Be Learning

Expand your capacity to understand and enjoy Life and Light.
Benefit from a good thing.
Undertake studies of new skills and languages.
Always be willing to learn to get ready for a world that yet exists.
Assume enrollment in classes that delight and intrigue you.
Embark upon a journey
of exploration, discovery and accomplishment.

I... am learning.

I like learning!

learn*ing *v.t.* 1. to acquire knowledge of or skill in by study, instruction or experience: *to learn French.* 2. to become informed of or acquainted with; ascertain: *to learn the truth.* 3. to gain (*a habit, mannerisms, attitudes, etc.*) by experience, exposure to example, or the like; acquire.

Be Leisurely

Allow yourself to include the peace of relaxation,
and the relaxation of peace
in your routine of activities and appearances.
Remember, the show starts only when you arrive.
So... enjoy being comfortable in the audience or on stage.

I am leisurely!

lei*sure*ly *adj.* 1. acting, proceeding, or done without haste. 2. showing or suggesting ample leisure. 3. free from the demands of work or duty: *leisurely they walked down the beach.*

Be Liberated

Set yourself free by releasing the grip fear has on your attention.
Extricate yourself from difficult situations,
avoid becoming co-dependent.
Remove any sense of dread you may feel
by remembering passionate patience for your dreams...
and continue wishing and dreaming.
Your ability to move about "at will"
is a liberty acquired though experience
and no one can take it away from you.
Prevail in this state of mind.
"Don't tread on me!"

I am liberated!

lib*er*ate *adj.* 1. to set free, as from oppression; release. 2. to disengage; set free
from combination, as a gas.

Be Lieve

Own yourself today.
"Lieve" is a word, which means gladly and willingly desirous.
It also means dear one, beloved and treasured.
Enjoy hopeful living.
You are here to enjoy You... being You!

I'm... lieve!

lieve *adj.* 1. gladly; willingly. 2. willing; desirous. 3. dear; precious; cherished.
4. esteemed, venerated, honored. 4. from Eve.

Be Light-Hearted

Be buoyant, feel upbeat and remain optimistic.
Let uplifting confidence permeate your inner world
as well as the surrounding kingdom.
Take cheer in everyday activities.
What's so is... "So what!"
Be optimistic and let nothing disturb your peace of mind.

I feel light-hearted...

I am light-hearted!

light*heart*ed *adj.* carefree, cheerful; gay; debonair.

Be Listening

Pay attention to others when in conversation with them.
Take note of what they are saying and,
especially, of what they are not saying.
Then, ask them if your perceptions are correct.
Communication is, after all, a two way street.
In the spirit of counsel confirm your observations
and see if you're both seeing eye-to-eye.

I am listening!

lis*ten*ing *adj.* 1. giving attention for the purpose of hearing. 2. heeding or paying attention to what is said; obey (*often followed by to*): *I've told him repeatedly, but he isn't listening to me.* 3. to wait attentively for a specific result or sound (*usually followed by for*): *to be listening for the other shoe to drop; to be listening for the telephone; to be listening for the sounds of peace.*

Be Loving

Share feelings of affection and love.
Express good feelings
and experience affinities as often as you like.
Utilize all your senses and, apply love liberally
tenderly touching each of those you love
with warmth and gentle caress.
Learn to fall in love... forever.

I am loving!

lov*ing *adj.* 1. profoundly tender. 2. a feeling of warm personal attachment or deep affection as for a parent, child, friend, or lover. 3. passionately affectionate to a person in an appropriately adult way. – *syn.* LOVE, AFFECTION, DEVOTION all mean a deep and enduring emotional regard, usually for another person. LOVE may apply to various kinds of regard: the charity of a creator, reverent adoration toward God or toward a person, the relation of parent and child, the regard of friends for each other, romantic feelings for either sex, etc. AFFECTION is a fondness for persons of either sex, which is enduring and tender but calm. DEVOTION is an intense love for a steadfast, enduring loyalty to a person; it may also imply consecration to a cause.

Be Luminous

Allow the light of truth to shine through you clearly and lucidly.
Exemplify the best of the human condition.
Be so bright that you glow in the dark.
Be an inspiration for others.

I feel luminous... I am luminous!

lu*mi*nous *adj.* 1. radiating or emitting light: luminous paint. 2. reflecting or diffusing light. 3. intellectually brilliant. 4. clear; lucid.

Be Magical

Use creatively diverse techniques to produce effects,
which render the ordinary amazing and remarkable.
Enhance your life with a feel for the unique and unusual.
Synchronicity promotes feelings of living a charmed existence.
Prepare things ahead of time
and then present them upon demand.

I am... magical!

mag*ic*al *adj.* 1. the art of employing the powers of nature to produce effects apparently supernatural. 2. the talent for developing results seemingly brought about by unseen entities and forces. 3. the ability to distract the attention of others and produce effects or events without seeming effort: *he produced the hors d'oeuvre's magically.*

Be Magnetic

Display a strong, attractive power and charm.
Position all your positive thoughts and feelings up front
and deflect bad stuff to the rear,
to behind... where you can't see it.
Repel negative forces with an optimistic mastery.
Be smart enough to command only that which is worthy of you.

I feel magnetic...

I am magnetic!

mag*net*ic *adj.* 1. of, or pertaining to, a magnet or magnetism. 2. having the properties of a magnet. 3. capable of being magnetized or attracted by a magnet. 4. exerting a strong attractive power or charm: *His magnetic personality brought him riches beyond belief.*

Be Magnificent

There is nothing so great that you cannot become it.
There is nothing so grand that you cannot attain it.
Focus on the appreciable things and they'll multiply.
Heaven is the state of becoming more of...
a magnificent entity is a magnetic one...
attracting more magnificence.

I feel magnificent...

I am magnificent!

mag*nif*i*cent *adj.* 1. making a splendid appearance or show; of surpassing beauty, size, etc. 2. extraordinarily fine; superb: *Others saw her life to be magnificent.* 3. noble; sublime. 4. great; grand.

Be Mature

Maturity... is awareness of the responsibility of thinking.
Your mind... encompasses the fullness of your nature
when you entertain yourself with what you will....
Spirits reflect patterns of perfection.
To think is to create.
To feel is to participate.
To do both is to become fully human.

I am mature!

ma*ture *adj.* 1. complete in natural growth or development, as plant and animal forms. 2. fully developed in body or mind, as a person. 3. completed, perfected, or elaborated in full by the mind: *mature plans.*

Be Meditative

Take time to contemplate issues that matter most to you.
Make decisions with a clear mind.
Shift gears by going through neutral first.
Relaxing helps focus the mind.
And, don't fear going into reverse, even your car has this feature:
it's for you to get around the universe in.

I feel meditative...

I am meditative!

med*i*ta*tive *adj.* 1. given to, characterized by, or indicative of deep thought or meditation; contemplative. 2. obtaining a birds eye view of multiple perspectives, opinions or outcomes possible as a result of catalytic efforts; consequential thinking.

Be Meek

Feel gentle and kind.
Take a step back... then two steps forward. Repeat.
Put your best foot forward because there are gains to be made.
Represent goodness;
a healthy dose of humility through your words and actions.
Those who continue to learn will inherit the earth!

I feel meek...

I am meek!

meek *adj.* 1. humbly patient. 2. sublimely forbearing. 3. self-controlled when subjected to annoyance or provocation. 4. enduring.

Be Merry

Ask yourself, "Am I the light... or am I the light bulb?"
By wearing a lighthearted approach to working with others
you provide feelings of great joy within yourself.
Be filled with cheerfulness in being part of a team
and joyous in disposition toward shared enthusiasm for success.
Hum a cheery tune to yourself
and enjoy the spirit of mirth on Earth.
Be the Light of Love and the Love of Light.
Let laughter echo ever after.

I feel merry...

I am merry!

mer*ry *adj.* 1. full of cheerfulness or gaiety; joyous in disposition or spirit: *a merry little man.* 2. laughingly gay; mirthful; festively joyous; hilarious: *a merry time at the party.* 3. causing happiness; pleasant; delightful. 4. make merry, to be festive; celebrate; party.

Be Mighty

Be exceptional in your strength of character
while upholding truths and principles,
which act to promote life, happiness and the pursuit of liberty.
Many, for a long, long time
will recognize the reputation you create today.
Emphasize only the best in quality
as proceeding from your lips and your pen.

I feel might...

I am mighty!

might*y *adj.* 1. having, characterized by, or showing might or power. 2. of great size; huge: *a mighty oak.* 3. great in amount, extent, degree, or importance; exceptional: *a mighty accomplishment.*

Be Miracle-Minded

Believe occurrences take place in this world
which surpass all known human wherewithal.
Be open to that, which you do not understand.
Activate angel energy by being one for others.

I am miracle-minded!

mir*a*cle-mind*ed *adj.* 1. of the nature of a miracle; marvelous. 2. having or
seeming to have the power to work miracles. – *syn.* 1. wonderful, extraordinary.
2. MIRACULOUS, PRETERNATURAL, SUPERNATURAL refer to that which
seems to transcend the laws of nature. MIRACULOUS usually refers to an
individual event that apparently contravenes known laws governing the physical
universe: *a miraculous cure.* PRETERNATURAL suggests the possession
of supernatural gifts or qualities: *Dogs have a preternatural sense of smell.*
SUPERNATURAL suggests divine or superhuman properties: *supernatural aid in
battle.*

Be Modest

Temper your appetite with moderation.
Know when you feel full and honor that awareness.
Satisfaction is easily attained
when you honestly appreciate your personal levels of satiety.
Be free from ostentation, pretense or showy extravagance.

I am modest!

mod*est *adj.* 1. having or showing a moderate or humble estimate of one's merits,
importance, etc. 2. having or showing regard for decencies of behavior, speech,
dress, etc. appropriate to surrounding conditions or events.

Be Moral

Be concerned with conduct and principles,
which support truth, beauty and goodness.
Conform to those self-evident principles
rather than blindly to law, custom or superstition.
Keep an open mind and an open heart
as you listen to the inner self.
Let your morals ascend into mota;
mutually observed transactional attitudes.

I feel moral...

I am moral!

mor*al *adj.* 1. referring to generally accepted customs or conduct in current society. 2. upright, honest, virtuous, honorable; implying high standards of honesty and honorable dealings, and of methods used, especially in the professions or in business. 3. ethical. 4. a paradigm.

Be Motivated

Tempt yourself into action by imagining how you'll "feel"
having once accomplished your goals.
Create your own treats and incentives.
Flip the circuit breaker of courage into the on position.
Feel... the surge of emotional energy
empower your intentions with dynamic determination.
Recapture the resolve you went to bed with.

I feel motivated... I am motivated!

mo*ti*vat*ed *adj.* 1. prompt actions that determine volition; incentive. 2. orientate the self towards goals or objects of action. 3. inwardly urge movement toward desirable outcomes and results: *after hearing there were millions to be made, they became motivated.*

Be Myself

Above all else, be who you are.
Get acquainted with "all" of yourself.
There's only one of you,
and without you, total Supreme being-ness cannot exist.
Discern the "I am..." for yourself.

I feel myself...

I am... myself!

my*self *adj.* 1. self-determined. 2. conscious of uniqueness of identity. 3. self-recognizant through memory, consciousness and insight. 4. observer of the observer.

Be Mystical

A mystery is something secret
or nearly impossible to understand,
arousing curiosity through its obscure nature.
Maintain a grin from ear to ear
and many will wonder what you're up to.
Observe by combining reason and logic
with metaphors and myths
based upon strong moral foundations, examples and stories
of what the right thing is for you to do or believe.
Anchor your identity to a reality,
which renders obvious the darkest night.

I am mystical!

mys*ti*cal *adj.* 1. mystic; occult (*common-folk culture.*) 2. of, or pertaining to, mystics or mysticism; the beliefs, ideas, or mode of thought of mystics.
3. practicing the doctrine of an immediate spiritual intuition of thoughts believed to transcend ordinary understanding or of a direct, intimate union with God through contemplation of Love, Light and Life.

Be Natural

Exist in accordance with patterns of nature.
Embrace the intrinsic values
and naked constitution you were born with.
Discover inherent tendencies, talents and gifts
and develop honest "feeling" for them.
Being natural does not imply being normal.
Being normal is not natural.

I feel natural...

I am natural!

nat*u*ral *adj.* 1. of, or pertaining, to nature. 2. existing in, or formed by, nature. 3. in accordance with the principles of the universe, with all its phenomena. 4. in accordance with human nature including, but not limited to, biological and mental functions or the urges to satisfy their requirements. 5. being such because of one's inborn nature: *a natural mathematician.* 6. having real or physical existence.

Be Neighborly

Overcome the tendency for isolation in life
by being friendly, helpful and respectful.
Encourage a sense of community by promoting friendships.
Introduce yourself... and then listen as they do the same.
Learn to be both personal and impersonal;
tho' always be personal first, then impersonal.
Show qualities befitting a neighbor;
learn when to say yes... and when to say no.

I feel neighborly... I am neighborly!

neigh*bor*ly *adj.* 1. acting in accordance with getting along with those who live nearby. 2. being sensitive to other's requirements for living or privacy. 3. showing kindliness or helpfulness toward others.

Be Nice

Be amiably pleasant, kind, desirable and delightful.
Package and promote the most kissable best of yourself.
Learn to clothe both body and mind... with taste.
Get dressed with the best attitudes in your wardrobe.
Go ahead; put your cute on and be nice.

I feel I'm nice...

I am nice!

nice *adj.* 1. pleasing; agreeable; delightful: *a nice visit.* 2. amiably pleasant; kind.
3. characterized by or requiring great accuracy, precision, skill, or delicacy: nice
workmanship. 4. refined as to manners, language, etc. 5. virtuous; respectable;
decorous: *a nice girl and boy.* 6. carefully neat as to dress, habits, etc.

Be Nifty

Be clever in your wit
timely in your expressions and stylish in dress.
Be known for expressing
"your own" unique place in the universe.
Don't strain to avoid the obvious
when creating your particular joie de vivre.
Add a dash of this and a splash of that
to make a difference on any day or night.

I feel nifty...

I am nifty!

nif*ty *adj.* smart; stylish; fine; clever.

Be Noble

Constitute in your personality
that which is of a distinguishing quality of character.
Discern what is good, right, advantageous,
pleasing, beneficial and desirable.
Follow your path as it leads to a high regard
for life and the living.
Create a generous reputation for yourself to live up to.

I am noble!

no*ble *adj.* 1. distinguished by rank or title. 2. pertaining to persons so
distinguished. 3. of, belonging to, or constituting, a hereditary class possessing
special social or political status in a country or state; of, or pertaining to the
aristocracy. 4. of an exalted moral character or excellence. 5. imposing in
appearance; magnificent. 6. of an admirably high quality. 7. grand, lordly, splendid,
stately. — *syn.* NOBLE, HIGH-MINDED, MAGNANIMOUS agree in referring
to lofty principles and loftiness of mind or spirit. NOBLE implies a loftiness of
character or spirit that scorns the petty, mean, base, or dishonorable: *a noble
deed.* HIGH-MINDED implies having elevated principles and consistently adhering
to them: a high-minded pursuit of legal reforms. MAGNANIMOUS suggests
greatness of mind or soul, especially as manifested in generosity or in overlooking
injuries: magnanimous toward his former enemies.

Be Nourishing

Eat to live; don't just live to eat.
Strengthen the truth of beautiful richness within you
by endorsing that which is worthy to be part of you.
Supplement the body with good food
and excite the mind with good thought.
Open your heart and observe love in action
for spiritual nourishment.

I... am nourishing!

nour*ish*ing *adj.* 1. sustaining with food or nutriment. 2. strengthening or
promoting.

117

Be Novel

Be yourself.
Remain fresh in your outlook and original in your essence.
Choose to be relatively new and of a different kind.
Position yourself on the leading edge of your imagination.
Believe you are unique enough to pursue your dreams.
Hold onto those creations, which you feel are innovative
and package them in preparation for the marketplace.

I feel novel...

I am novel!

nov*el *adj.* 1. unprecedented; original; imaginative. 2. newest; latest; hot off the press. 3. up-to-the-minute; modernistic; avant-garde.

Be Nurturing

Promote development of your mind
and encourage the growth of your spirit.
Offer a helping hand to others,
by sharing the insight of your understanding and knowledge.
Provide the nourishment of truth, beauty, and goodness
for yourself and your loved ones.
Nurture mind, body and spirit into congruency with wisdom.

I feel nurturing...

I am nurturing!

nur*tur*ing *adj.* 1. to promote the development of by providing nourishment, support, encouragement, etc., during the stages of growth. 2. to bring up; educate; train.

Be Observant

Be quick to notice and sharp to perceive.
There's a wall of monitors in your mind
facing you and begging for your attention.
Pay attention to the monitor most important to your poise,
keep both sets of eyes – open and on the road.
Let peripheral vision provide you with an E.S.P.-like alertness.
Be conscious of consequential thinking and go time traveling.
Sequential thinking
offers the insight needed to get you to where you want to go next.

I am observant!

I'm... observant!

ob*serv*ant *adj.* 1. observing or regarding attentively; watchful. 2. quick to notice or perceive; alert. 3. careful in observing the spirit of a law, custom, religious ritual, or the like.

Be Olympic

Go for the gold.
Keep your eyes on the prize.
Picture your success
with visionary clarity and heartfelt accuracy.
Study muscle memory and visual motor rehearsal.
Participate in the development
of your mind, talents, and treasures
as if you were going to compete
in Olympic games and festivities in the near future.

I am Olympic!

o*lym*pic *adj.* pertaining to games and festivities consisting of athletic and sports contests involving amateur participants from nations throughout the world, held every four years, each time in a different country, from 776 B.C.E.

Be Omniscient

Through the "I Am," observe your connection with all that is.
Through the "Here and Now,"
watch yourself slipping through the portal called eternity.
Ancient wisdom within you
sounds the bell of truth as it is revealed.
Hook up with the infinite potential
of the unified quantum field, "the grid," that is this universe.
Be able to identify your quantum neighborhood.
Monitor the mystery that is you and your life.

I am omniscient!

I feel omniscient!

om*nis*cient *adj.* 1 having complete or infinite knowledge, awareness, or understanding; perceiving all things. 2. having extensive knowledge: *Goethe was omniscient in his era.*

Be Open-Hearted

Be unreserved in your welcome,
candid in your observations and frank with your feelings.
Keep the lore of your love available.
Let your character remain intact
within a seemingly impersonal world.
Emboss the texture of love onto the fabric of your soul
as you weave the threads of your intentions
tenderly and with care.

I feel open-hearted...

I am open-hearted!

o*pen-heart*ed *adj.* 1. unreserved, candid, or frank: open-hearted advice.
2. kindly; benevolent: *an open-hearted gift to charity.*

Be Open-Minded

Recognize how wonderfully
processes of thinking and contents of thought flow
when you are friendly to new ideas and arguments.
Be unprejudiced in your perceptions.
Let your access to mind
be like a satellite dish: open and receptive.
Turn the knob of your attention,
tuning into that which is true, beautiful and good.
Once again, the mind is like a parachute
... it only works when it is open.

I... am open-minded!

o*pen-mind*ed *adj.* 1. having or showing a mind receptive to new ideas or
arguments. 2. unprejudiced.

Be Optimal

Be the best and most desirable you that you can be.
Choose to orient yourself toward tasty results
and rewards that you feel are well worth the effort.
Let efficiency be one of the qualifiers for your intentions.
Operate like a smooth running machine with energy to spare
and very little wear and tear on the moving parts.

I feel optimal...

I am optimal!

op*ti*mal *adj.* best; most desirable, long lasting.

Be Optimistic

Possess the propensity for taking the favorable viewpoint in life.
Positivity is the secret energy applied when reaching for success.
Promise yourself to be so strong
that nothing can disturb your peace of mind.
Promote hope!
Reflect on possibilities with feelings of hopefulness.
Don't worry, be convinced.

I feel great when I'm being optimistic...

I am optimistic!

op*ti*mis*tic *adj.* 1. disposed to take a favorable view of happenings or possibilities. 2. reflecting optimism: *an optimistic plan.*

Be Organized

Put yourself into a state
of physical and mental competence and order,
prepared to perform the task at hand.
Know where things are:
a place for everything and everything returned to its' place.
Start projects by first reading any and all
plans, instructions and procedure manuals
or by watching the lastest greatest info-gizmo.
Get all the material in order
and then follow directions step-by-step
until you've completed your endeavor.

I feel organized...

I am organized!

or*gan*ized *adj.* 1. formed into a whole consisting of interdependent or coordinated parts: *an organized committee.* 2. systemized: *the office files are organized.*

Be Original

Belong to the beginning thought: the "I Am...!"
Command yourself to be... with each moment that arrives:
inventive and creative.
Feel the Source surge through you...
sustaining fresh channels for new ideas.
After all... you are a new you, each and every day.
Prevent peer pressure from changing you
into something you're not.

I feel original...

I am original!

o*rig*i*nal *adj.* 1.belonging, or pertaining, to the origin or beginning of something, or to a thing at its beginning. 2. having originality; inventive or creative: *an original thinker.* 3. showing originality; new; fresh: *an original viewpoint.* 4. noting the first presentation, performance, or version of something. 5. being that from which a copy, a translation, or the like is made.

Be Outstanding

Seek to perform skillfully with your talents.
Earn a place in prominence
showcasing **you** pleasantly; conspicuously.
Excel within your chosen field of study, discipline or hobby.
Get outside the norm... by outfoxing the fox.

I feel outstanding...

I... am outstanding!

out*stand*ing *adj.* 1. prominent or conspicuous; striking. 2. continuing in existence. 3. (*of capital stocks*) issued and sold or in circulation. 4. standing out; projecting; detached.

123

Be Passionate

Embrace enthusiasm intensely
with e-motion sparked within your soul.
Spread passionate feelings...
like liquid wildfire on a butter knife
throughout your body, mind and spirit.
Radiate the glow of desire; touch the fabric of your dreams.
Inhale deeply... experience ardent fever.

I feel passionate... I am passionate!

pas*sion*ate *adj.* 1. influenced or dominated by intense emotion or strong feeling: *a passionate advocate for socialism.* 2. expressing or revealing strong emotion. 3. having or revealing intense enthusiasm. 4. easily affected with or influenced by desire.

Be Patient

Impatience is poison to the spirit.
You can't be happy or in bliss if your spirit is poisoned.
You are an eternal being... you will be around for a long time.
What else simply has to be done right now...
other than being here now... wherever you are?
Persevere through intolerance
and uncertainty, pain and discomfort,
with minimal complaint, rage or anger
by adopting patience as your approach to life.
Don't allow tour-guides for guilt trips
to entertain you (real or imagined.)
Overcome feelings of despair
and master disappointment disabilities
by observing the larger picture,
(take a few steps back and have another look.)
And remember,
you are not alone in your endurance of any passing event.
A future "you," is also encouraging you to keep on... keeping on.

I feel patient... I am patient!

pa*tient *adj.* 1. bearing annoyance, pain, etc. without complaint or anger. 2. an ability or willingness to suppress annoyance when confronted with delay: *to be patient with a child who is a slow learner.* – *syn.* 1. composed, self-possessed. 2. PATIENCE, ENDURANCE imply qualities of calmness, stability, and persistent courage in trying circumstances. PATIENCE may denote calm, self-possessed, and un-repining bearing of pain, misfortune, annoyance, or delay; or painstaking and untiring industriousness or (less often) application in the doing of something: *to bear afflictions with patience.* ENDURANCE denotes the ability to bear exertion, hardship, or suffering (*without implication of moral qualities required or shown*): *a marathon requires great endurance.*

Be Peaceful

Be inclined to prefer the absence of strife and dissension.
Proceed from a tranquil state of mind seeking paths of harmony.
Act now to promote peace in your personal sphere of existence.
Then help others seeking peace in their orb as well.

I feel peaceful... I am peaceful!

peace*ful *adj.* 1. characterized by peace; free from strife or disorder. 2. of, pertaining to, or characteristic of a state or time of peace. 3. peaceable; not argumentative. – *syn.* PEACEFUL, PLACID, SERENE, TRANQUIL refer to what is characterized by lack of strife or agitation. PEACEFUL today is rarely applied to persons; it refers to situations, scenes and activities free of disturbances or occasionally, of warfare: *a peaceful life.* PLACID, SERENE, and TRANQUIL are used mainly of persons; when used of things (*usually elements of nature*) there is a touch of personification. PLACID suggests an unruffled calm that verges on complacency: *a placid disposition; a placid stream.* SERENE is a somewhat nobler word; when used of persons it suggests dignity, composure, and graciousness: *a serene old man and woman; when applied to nature there is a suggestion of mellowness: the serene landscapes of autumn.* TRANQUIL implies a command of emotions, often because of strong faith, that keeps a person unagitated even in the midst of excitement or danger.

Be Perceptive

Use your second sight.
See without the external eyes and listen to the inner voice.
Let insight and understanding guide you.
First is vision, and then peripheral vision
followed by feelings of intuition.
Discern spirit
and its destiny by opening both inner eye and ear.
Be smart enough to find clues for success
on this "scavenger-hunt-like" life.

I am perceptive!

per*cep*tive *adj.* 1. having the power or faculty of perceiving. 2. of, pertaining to, or showing apprehension by means of the senses or of the mind; cognition; understanding. 3. having or showing keenness of insight, or intuition.

Be Persevering

Persist in what you choose to undertake.
Maintain a feeling of purpose to sustain your dreams.
Your dreams and visions
are the guiding light to a future here and now.
Exercise courage
and overcome depression disabilities through positivity.
Each morning awaken with an invitation to a brand new day:
by saying to yourself,
"Something great is going to happen today... I know it is!"
(Repeat as required.)

I am persevering!

per*se*ver*ing *adj.* displaying perseverance; persistent; steadfast: *a persevering student.*

Be Personable

Feel likable and outgoing...
others like themselves better in your presence.
Place your personality before impersonality
in approaching or working with others.
Give people the gift of warm ambiance and friendly charisma.
Remember, love is the secret
to beneficial association between personalities.
Experience an emotional depth of meaning
for all things that matter.

I feel personable...

I am personable!

per*son*a*ble *adj.* 1. of pleasing personal appearance; handsome or comely; attractive. 2. socially desirable.

Be Physical

Give your body the nourishment and activity it needs
to breathe and sustain the life you choose to embrace.
Let your actions provide tangible experiences for you.
Know you've been somewhere; touch it.
Manipulate reality by getting physical with it, feel it.

I feel physical...

I am physical!

phys*i*cal *adj.* 1. of, or pertaining to, the body: *physical exercise.* 2. of, or pertaining to, that which is material: *the physical universe.* 3. of, or pertaining to, the properties of matter and energy other than those peculiar to living matter: *physical science.*

Be Pioneering

Be the first and original in your pursuits.
Be adventurous
and pave the trail with notes and records for others.
Go where you believe others seldom go
and see the place for the first time.
If anyone can accomplish his or her dream, you can.

I am pioneering!

pi*o*neer*ing *adj.* 1. being the earliest, original, first of a particular kind, etc.:
a pioneering method of adult education. 2. of, pertaining to, or characteristic of
a pioneer or pioneers. 3. being the earliest in any field of inquiry, enterprise, or
progress.

Be Playful

Liberate your frolicsome nature
and release your aptitudes for inner happiness.
Play is the art of aimlessly pursuing pleasurable activities.
Evoke the uninhibited part of your childhood
and re-establish this vital connection with your core being.
Utilize youthful energy to balance life.
Take pleasure in delightful pastimes.

I feel playful...

I am playful!

play*ful *adj.* 1. full of play; sportive; frolicsome. 2. pleasantly humorous or teasing:
a playful remark.

Be Pleasant

Be agreeable in conversation and enjoyable in presence.
Cultivate an amiable personality with polite manners
and a highly refined social disposition.
You know you're cool,
so let others discover it as well and enjoy this part of you.
Remember... realize when it's time to leave your audience;
wanting more.

I feel pleasant...

I am pleasant!

pleas*ant *adj.* 1. pleasing, agreeable, or enjoyable: *pleasant news; pleasant weather.* 2. (*of persons, manners, disposition, etc.*) socially acceptable or adept; polite; amiable.

Be Poetic

Endow your thoughts and expressions with a creative flair.
Express from your heart the beauty and depth felt
when to the essence of life you commit yourself.
Let the lilt in each step spark poetic inner 'flections on life.
Relish the rhythmic recall of rhymes, reasons,
times and seasons.

I am poetic!

I feel poetic!

po*et*ic *adj.* 1. possessing the qualities or charm of poetry. 2. characteristic of, or befitting, a poet. 3. endowed with the faculty or feeling of a person who has the gift of poetic speech, thought, imagination and creation, together with eloquence of expression: *a poetic eulogist.* 4. having or showing the sensibility of a poet: *a poetic lover.*

129

Be Poised

Stand up straight, hold your head up high,
pull your shoulders back and let them drop;
this is your perfect posture.
Inhale deeply through your nose --
let oxygen fill the balloons of your lungs --
then release slowly through pursed lips.
Be ready for action
and maintain a state of balance with a sense for equilibrium.
Carry your "Self" with assurance and confidence.
Command your attitude to be composed
with feelings of dignity and positive expectations

I feel poised... I am poised!

poised *adj.* 1. (*of a person*) composed, dignified, and self-assured. 2. being in balance or equilibrium. 3. hovering or suspended in midair. 4. self-confident manner or bearing; self-possessed.

Be Positive

Positivity is the most powerful weapon we have for waging peace.
Proceed in a direction
that's potentially most possible, beneficial and progressive.
Emphasize that which is laudable, hopeful and desirable.
Retain unconditional confidence in the collective movement
of the Universe toward the age of Life and Light.
Supplant the inferior with the superior.
Accentuate the affirmative.

I am positive!

pos*i*tive *adj.* 1. explicit; definite. 2. determined by enactment or convention; arbitrarily laid down: *positive law.* 3 admitting of no question: *positive proof.*
4. confident in an opinion or assertion. 5. consisting in, or characterized by, the presence or possession of distinguishing or marked qualities or features
(*as opposed to negative*): *Light is positive, darkness is negative.*

Be Possible

Hold onto your dreams and fantasies
and dwell upon them as something that can happen.
You are the modeling clay,
forming and modifying yourself to your delight.
Stimulate your mind to create that which you require.
Identify what you need, want and desire... write it down.

I feel possible...

I am possible.

pos*si*ble *adj.* 1. that may or can exist, happen, be done or be used, etc.
2. that may be true or may be the case: *It's possible he went that way.*

Be Powerful

Within the constitution of your nature...
remember your personal history of strength and endurance.
Command the attention of people and resources needed
by building on all that has brought you to this moment.
Take those character traits and qualities,
which reflect truth, beauty and goodness
and aggregate them into a rock solid position of prominence.

I... am powerful!

I feel... powerful!

pow*er*ful *adj.* 1. having or exerting great power or force. 2. physically and/or
mentally strong, as a person. 3. producing great physical effects, as a machine or
a blow. 4. potent; efficacious: *a powerful drug.* 5. having great effectiveness, as a
speech, speaker, reason, etc.: *a powerful delivery of a very timely speech.*

Be Prepared

Put thoughts and matters into proper perspective and condition.
Maintain readiness and familiarize yourself
with that which is to be both expected and unexpected.
Over time, recognize what it takes to be successful.
Get ready for your days and set up for your nights,
to better enjoy peace, health and prosperity.

I am prepared!

pre*pared *adj.* put in readiness; get ready.

Be Present

Observe such presence of mind
that you are wide-awake, alert and self-possessed.
Continue your relationships
with aplomb, composure and steadfastness.
Exercise self-reliance and self-control.
Make sure the minds' circuit breakers
for intuition, understanding and knowledge,
courage, counsel, worship and wisdom
are in the on position... for the "I Am..." to show up.
Balance your approach toward life
with a sang-froid, cool disposition.
Allow courage of common sense room to create a sane point of view.
Keep your head while it may seem all about you are losing theirs.

I am present!

pres*ent *adj.* 1 being, existing, or occurring at this time or now. 2. at this time: *articles for present use.* 3. being here and now rather than elsewhere.

Be Productive

Display powers of performance.
Cause, and bring about,
thoughts and things you work so hard for.
Your mental characteristics display magnetic influences.
Often harsh, the only fair way to gauge anything is by results.
What you choose to practice today
will be brought forth tomorrow: fruitfully so.
Pull treasures from the past
and buff them up for brand-new appeal... once again.

I am productive!

pro*duc*tive *adj.* 1 having the power of producing. 2. producing readily or abundantly: *a productive vineyard.* 3. producing or tending to produce goods and services having exchange value.

Be Professional

Polish your attitudes
into being the professional leader you dream yourself to be.
Be willing to operate on a level
commensurate with your best abilities.
Offer choices reflecting professionalism
to your team of associates.
Exude the essence of personal proficiency,
organizational moxie and team reliability.

I feel professional... I am professional!

pro*fes*sion*al *adj.* 1. engaged in an activity as a means of livelihood or for gain: *a professional golfer; a professional potter.* 2. of, pertaining to, or connected with a profession: *professional studies.* 3. appropriate to a profession or to professions: *professional attitudes.* 4. engaged in one of the learned professions: *a professional man or woman.* 5. competent; expert.

Be Progressive

Be one to advocate progress
within technology, sociology, theory-ology and be-ology.
Be forward thinking
and excited about possibilities, potentialities and probabilities.
You're only on this planet for a short time so make the best of it.
Then, as you move on, you'll be ready for bigger challenges.

I feel progressive...

I am progressive!

pro*gres*sive *adj.* 1. of, pertaining to, or characterized by progress. 2. advocating progress, as in technology or politics. 3. progressing; advancing; improving: *a progressive community.* 4. of, pertaining to, or following methods of progressive education: *a progressive school.*

Be Prolific

Put a lot of irons in the fire
and keep a close watch over the ones in back.
Abundant productivity
"is" within the blueprint of your capabilities.
So, produce liberally, with care and efficiency.
Life is, after all, a plethora of tasty, tasty fruits.
If not one thing... go after another.

I feel prolific...

I am... prolific!

pro*lif*ic *adj.* 1. producing offspring, young, fruit, etc., abundantly. 2. characterized by abundant productivity.

134

Be Proportional

Size is relative.
Adjust your perspective
to observe love and beauty in harmony and balance.
Integrate the spheres of your body, mind and spirit
with symmetry.
Superimpose your mind upon divine ideals
and spirit worthy adventures of size and consideration.

I feel proportional...

I am proportional!

pro*por*tion*al *adj.* 1. having or being in proportion. 2. of, or pertaining to, proportion; relative.

Be Prosperous

Handle your success, wealth and welfare with comfort.
Acknowledge the richness of your life
and the good fortune you find.
From riches receive riches and yet riches remain.
Acquire what you need when you need it.
Believe you're worthy of prosperity.

I feel prosperous...

I am prosperous!

pros*per*ous *adj.* 1. having or characterized by good fortune, success, or wealth. 2. favorable or propitious.

Be Proud

Think well of your accomplishments
in building and achieving a character having impeccable quality.
Be well pleased and appreciate being satisfied
at the time success is happening.
Let your emotions
reflect feelings of pride in your heart and stand proud.
Promote recognition of excellence within yourself.

I feel proud...

I am proud!

proud *adj.* 1. thinking well of one's self because of one's accomplishments,
possession, etc. 2. feeling honored, as by a distinction conferred on one.
3. governed in one's words or actions by self-respect. 4. promoting a feeling of
pride: *a proud moment.* 5. stately, majestic, or distinguished.

Be Prudent

Be judicious and careful in your affairs.
Provide for the future by managing resources in the present.
Wisdom is the ability
to do today, what will be required tomorrow.
You get to sleep in the bed you make
so make sure it's worthy of you.
Learn to save 10% of all you earn for yourself...
not to spend later... but to build financial net worth.

I am prudent!

pru*dent *adj.* 1. judicious or wisely cautious in practical affairs. 2. careful in
providing for the future; provident.

Be Purposeful

Acquire a motive worthy of you: a mota.*
Establish your hero's journey and touch each day as it arrives.
Determine for yourself what you want
and begin taking those steps
to achieve the next steps thereafter, and so forth.
Get your motor running.

I feel purposeful...

I am purposeful!

pur*pose*ful *adj*. 1. having a reason for which something exists or happens. 2. determined; resolute. 3. full of meaning; significant. (*Ed. Note.* *mota is an acronym for <u>m</u>utually <u>o</u>bserved <u>t</u>ransactional <u>a</u>ttitudes.)

Be Quality

Be conscious of superior thinking,
excellence in feeling and considerations rich in value.
Demonstrate an appealing character,
high in worthiness in both thought and action.
Enjoy the distinction of having personal attributes,
that are great, noble and admirable.
Are you being taught quality?

I recognize quality...

I am quality!

qual*i*ty *adj*. 1. a characteristic, property, or attribute. 2. character of nature, as belonging to or distinguishing a thing: *the quality of a sound*. 3. character with respect to fineness, or grade of excellence: *food of fabulous quality*.

Be Questioning

Cultivate an alert and curious mind.
Let your intellectual pursuits help you discover who you are,
why things are the way they are,
and why you are here in the first place.
Take advantage of counsel in your affairs.
And, don't be afraid to put people on the spot in your search
for truth, beauty and goodness;
nothing ever remains hidden for long.

I am questioning!

ques*tion*ing *adj.* 1 indicating or implying a question: *a questioning tone.*
2. characterized by, or indicating, intellectual curiosity; inquiring: *an alert and questioning mind.*

Be Radiant

An ambiance of good health shines ever more brightly
as you top it off with a smile.
Emote rays of hope and joy.
Emit light from the twinkling of your eyes.
Let others wonder what you're thinking about.
"What's so amusing?"

I feel radiant...

I am radiant!

ra*di*ant *adj.* 1. emitting rays of light; shining; bright. 2. bright with joy, hope, etc.
3. projecting warmth and cheery brightness. (*Ed. Note.* emote has a similar root in the word emotion: *To emote is to feel out loud, radiating emotions* (*usually in positive tones; happiness, etc.*)

Be Rational

You are endowed with faculties of good thought and reasoning.
Exercise it;
show good judgment and "common" sense in traffic for instance.
Don't beat your head against the wall...
use inner consideration and external counsel to sort things out.
Act as one blessed with a mind;
reach for reasonable conclusions
and sensible connections for understanding.

I am rational!

ra*tion*al *adj.* 1. agreeable to, or in accord with, reason; reasonable; sensible.
2. having or exercising reason, sound judgment or good sense. 3. being in full
possession of one's reason; sane; lucid: *The patient appeared to be perfectly
rational.* 4. endowed with the faculty of reason: *Man is a rational animal.*

Be Ready

Be prepared and in fit condition,
geared-up for immediate response and action.
If you've never become familiar
with the courage of being ready at all,
how do you expect to feel ready when it's required?
Find that place inside yourself, where you know you're ready,
and access it when needed.
Don't hesitate; be willing to get ready.

I feel ready... I am ready!

read*y *adj.* 1. completely prepared, in fit condition or immediately available for
action or use. 2. willing or not hesitant: *ready to forgive.* 3. prompt or quick
in perceiving, comprehending, speaking, writing, etc. 4. proceeding from or
showing such quickness: *a ready reply.* 5. prompt or quick in action, performance,
manifestation, etc.: *a keen mind and ready wit.* 6. inclined; disposed; apt: *not too
ready to criticize others.* 7. in such a condition as to be imminent; likely at any
moment: *a leaf ready to fall.*

Be Real

Choose to be genuine and authentic.
Don't be false, misleading or counterfeit.
Have an actual, rather than an imaginary existence.
Stop pretending.

I feel real...

I am real!

re*al *adj.* 1. being actually such; not merely so-called: *a real victory.* 2. sincere or unfeigned: *a real friend; real sympathy.* 3. true; not merely ostensible or nominal: *real events.*

Be Reasonable

Choose to be agreeable to
and in accordance with reason, logic and insight.
Be rational in your understandings
and acknowledge the considerations of your peers.
For meaning to take place in your world
there must be some depth and breadth to it.
Take your insights
and weigh them according to this form of council.

I feel reasonable...

I am reasonable!

rea*son*a*ble *adj.* 1. not exceeding the limit prescribed by reason; not excessive: *reasonable terms.* 2. capable of rational behavior, decision.

Be Reborn

Renew your existence through growth.
Experience personal renaissance
by letting go of who you think you are
for who you think you can become.
You are embarking upon a fascinating journey,
an inward and upward ascension.
Take each day as it comes
and find upon awakening, survival of another night.

I feel reborn...

I am reborn!

re*born *adj.* 1. having undergone a new or second birth; renewed existence,
activity, or growth. 2. renaissance; revival.

Be Receptive

Be open to suggestions and ideas,
able to access knowledge and information;
inclined to intelligently admit
both constructive criticism and compliments.
Open the doors of your mind and heart with welcoming arms
and harbor "thought-ships" worthy of your ports of call.
In obedience to the Law of Attraction
you must become ready to receive.

I feel receptive...

I am receptive!

re*cep*tive *adj.* 1. having the quality of receiving, taking in, or admitting. 2. able or
quick to receive knowledge, ideas, etc. 3. willing or inclined to receive suggestions,
offers, etc. 4. of, or pertaining to, reception or receptors. (*Ed. Note.* Law of
Attraction, where *Thoughts become Things,* is as certain and powerful as the Law
of Gravity.)

Be Reciprocal

Be complementary in your affairs.
Give, perform and feel in turn with others.
Decide upon equal footing in your relationships.
Graduate from the theory of return-on-investment
to the supernal concept of giving without thought of return.

I am reciprocal!

re*cip*ro*cal *adj.* 1. given or felt by each toward the other; mutual. 2. given, performed, felt, etc., in return. 3. giving or receiving in like spirit.

Be Rejoicing

Commemorate your blessings.
Choose to observe and celebrate truth, beauty and goodness.
Take delight in your associations and relationships,
bringing joy to the lives of others
through your feelings of gladness.
Share your sense of beauty in the way you are.
Ring the tuning fork of truth by simply being yourself.
Bubble over with happiness
and express good cheer with laughter.

I feel like rejoicing...

I am rejoicing!

re*joic*ing *v. i.* to be glad; take delight (*often followed by in*): *to be rejoicing in another's happiness.* – *v. t.* to be making joyful; en-gladdening.

Be Relaxed

Be free from the long-term effects of tension
and feelings of anxiety.
Train your body and mind
to let go of the daily demands placed upon them.
Develop various methods to help you relax
so you can spring back into the swing of things.
Re-energize yourself by putting up your feet and resting.

I feel relaxed...

I am relaxed!

re*laxed *adj.* 1. to be made less tense, rigid, or firm; made lax. 2. to be diminished in the force of (*effort, attention, etc.*). 3. to have been made less strict or severe, as in rules or discipline. 4. to have released or brought relief from the effects of tension, anxiety, etc. 5. to have attained peace of mind.

Be Reliable

Remember; do what you say you're going to do.
Choose to be trustworthy
and predispose your character to be honest.
And, when made part of a team,
do your best... for the edification of the whole team.
Others need to feel you can be depended upon.

I'm reliable!

re*li*a*ble *adj.* that which may be relied upon; trustworthy.

143

Be Remarkable

Let your actions and appearances speak well of you
and others will speak in like kind.
Give consent to living an amazing and distinguished life.
Sanction significant achievements with patience.
Endeavor to be worthy of notice.

I feel remarkable...

I am remarkable!

re*mark*a*ble *adj.* 1. notably unusual; extraordinary. 2. worthy of notice.

Be Resilient

Choose to spring back
from exhaustion, illness, depression and adversity.
Resume your life with feelings of wholeness
and a sense of purpose.
Defeat disappointment disability
by not making a mountain out of a molehill.
There's no law in the universe
that requires you to entertain pain and bad psychodramas.
You have much better things to do
than to lay around sick all day
or go diving into the negative looking for its positive side.

Get up, get up... get up!

I am resilient!

re*sil*ient *adj.* 1. springing back; rebounding. 2. returning to the original form or position after being bent, compressed, or stretched out of shape. 3. recovering readily; buoyant.

Be Resolute

Be firmly resolved and self-determined.
Choose to continue on... steadfast in the resolution
that you'll climb each step to the very top...
of each mountain or ladder.
When you've reached these heights of viewpoints
observe how much better off you are
because you did much more than just try.
Make up your mind... so your dreams of climbing ladders
and visions from mountain tops come true.

I am resolute!

res*o*lute *adj.* 1. firmly settled upon by deliberate choice and will. 2. characterized by firmness and determination (*to do something*).

Be Resonic

Vibrate like a speaker cone.
Don't participate with the silent majority.
Stir up that nest of sleeping giants by throwing a tone at it.
A ripple on the water means a pebble's in the pond.
Social progress often comes from the genius of one person.

I feel resonic...

I am resonic!

re*son*ic *adj.* able to write or vibrate; to speak out; shock others into awareness.

Be Resourceful

Deal skillfully and promptly with new people and situations.
Use that, which is available to you
to overcome difficulties and solve problems,
whether seen or unforeseen.
Recognize value in things others throw away.
The Source and Center of all that is... after all...
remains Resourceful.

I am resourceful!

re*source*ful *adj.* 1. exercising the ability to do something well, from talent through practice and training. 2. develop competent excellence in performance with thoughts and things at your immediate disposal. 3. perform repeatedly; recycle.

Be Responsible

Be directly answerable
for the effects of your thoughts and actions.
Accept the consequences for what you've caused to bring about.
Be response enabled and able to respond, response-able.
Take ownership of your life.

I feel responsible...

I am responsible!

re*spon*si*ble *adj.* 1. answerable or accountable, as for something within one's power or control. 2. involving accountability or responsibility: *a responsible position.* 3. chargeable with being the author, cause, or occasion of something (*usually followed by for*). 4. having a capacity for moral decisions and therefore accountable. 5. able to discharge obligations or repay debts.

Be Responsive

Allow your self to hear, think, feel and see.
Act when the universe delivers opportunities
for your dreams to come true.
Be ready to observe questions and answers:
reply within the spirit intended.
Either be excited about being on board the relation-ship
or get off at the next port.
Dance... or get off the floor.

I feel responsive... I am responsive!

re*spon*sive *adj.* making answer or reply, especially responding or reacting readily
to influences, appeals, efforts, etc.

Be Rewarding

Recognize results and acknowledge those results
no matter the source of their accomplishment...
whether they belong to you or someone else.
At the end of any movie is a listing of credits
for anyone and everyone who helped in making it happen.
Your life is like a movie... how many people are on your list?
Give others the credit they're due.
Compensate them with Fruits of the Spirit...
which are indeed tasty, and wholly nourishing.
And, most of all... pat "you" on the back for coming this far.
Then, do a Snoopy Dog dance
as you copiously achieve your dreams
and... let electric bliss exist in your body, mind and spirit
... right here... right now.

I am rewarding!

re*ward*ing *adj.* 1. giving value in return for service, merit, etc. 2. recompensing
or requiting (*a person or animal*) for service, merit, achievement, etc.

Be Rhythmical

Feel movement swaying within each moment.
Syncopate movement of body
with the melody and harmony of your spirit.
Embody a sense of natural movement and timing.
Grasp a feel for the ticking of today's background cadence
and word it to the downbeat.
Sail away with the music.

I feel rhythmical...

I am rhythmical!

rhyth*mi*cal *adj.* 1. periodic, as motion, a drumbeat, etc. 2. having a flowing
rhythm of pattern: *an excellent rhythmical sense.*

Be Romantic

Express the amorous emotions you feel
and celebrate the nature of love.
Subordinate form to content
and encourage free will to express the heart.
Woo the object of your attention
with carefully designed, well-thought-out action.
Partake in the adventure of love
by observing the ideals of mutual passion.

I feel romantic...

I am romantic!

ro*man*tic *adj.* 1. imbued by idealism, a desire for adventure, etc. 2. characterized
by a preoccupation with love or by the idealizing of love or one's beloved.
3. displaying or expressing love. 4. ardent; passionate; fervent. 5. encouraging
freedom of emotional treatment, imagination, and introspection, and often
celebrating nature, the common man and woman, and freedom of spirit.

Be Savvy

Be a step ahead.
Know a lot but understand more.
Sharpen your perception and intuition with peripheral vision.
Whet your senses by having peripheral feeling.
Acquire essential information
and use insight to further attract your goals.

I am savvy!

sav*vy *adj.* understanding; intelligence; insight.

Be Scintillating

Shine your smile and sparkle your eyes.
On the canvas of your face place a slim grin.
In the chalice of your heart feel effervescent cheer
and let goodness bubble forth and over.
Permit your mind to captivate others... brilliantly.

Right on!

I feel scintillating...

I am scintillating!

scin*til*la*ting *adj.* 1. to emit sparks. 2. to sparkle; flash: *a mind scintillating with brilliance.* 3. to twinkle, as the stars.

Be Secure

Don't worry... be certain!
Choose to be free in your choices.
Do whatever it takes to be safe and enjoy your privacy.
Believe in yourself and have confidence in your environment.

I feel secure... I am secure!

se*cure *adj.* 1. free from or not exposed to danger; safe. 2. dependable; firm; not liable to fail, yield, become displaced, etc. as a support or a fastening: *The building was secure even in an earthquake.* 3. affording safety, as a place: *He needed a secure hiding place.* 4. in safe custody or keeping: *Here in the vault the necklace was secure.* 5. free from care; without anxiety: *emotionally or financially secure.*

Be Seeing

You... are the observer.
Look around, watch, and perceive,
in order to understand more clearly.
Seeing helps believing,
so focus your intuition
and edify both your courage and knowledge.
The insight of your environment
reflects the world you imagine it to be.
You are in command of the perspective filters you use.
Master both inner and outer eyes.
Observe Life and Light with Your ancient wisdom!

I am seeing!

see*ing *adj.* 1. perceive mentally; discern; understand: *seeing the point of the argument.* 2. to construct a mental image of: *He was seeing his father as he was 25 years ago.* 3. to be cognizant of; recognize: *She saw charming traits in not-so-charming people.*

Be Seeking

It is the question that leads to answers.
Learn to identify the quest,
then state it out loud,
or as quietly as you please, in the form of a question.
Join the cycle of asking, searching, finding and receiving.
Discover your own rites of passage.
Ask and you shall receive.
Make your requests... say your prayers.

I am seeking!

seek*ing *adj.* 1. going in search of or quest of: *seeking the truth.* 2. finding or discovering by searching or questioning: *seeking the solution to a problem.* 3. asking for; requesting.

Be Self-Assured

Familiarize yourself with faith, reliance and positive certainty.
Trust these qualities to be inherent character traits
and develop internal dialogues with yourself, with confidence.
In these discussions with yourself
assert your value and feelings of worthiness.
Tell yourself stories
revealing knowledge, understanding and self-counsel;
this observation brings relief from the stress of the unknown.

I feel self-assured...

I am self-assured!

self-as*sured *adj.* self-confident.

151

Be Self-Controlled

Exercise appropriate hold
over your actions, feelings and emotions,
recognizing too when it is most appropriate to do so.
Self-possession carries with it
the ability for constructive re-development.
When necessary apply the brakes of moderation in all things.
Take command of your life-ship and be your own tour guide.

I feel self-controlled...

I am self-controlled!

self-con*trolled *adj.* control or constraint of oneself, of one's actions, feelings or emotions.

Be Self-Esteemed

Observe a personal set of values,
and respect that only you can say who and how you are.
Toot your horn for yourself
and let love sparkle showers of laughter in your perceptions
and that of any audience.
Take pleasure in knowing...
you know... how much... you're truly worth.

I feel self-esteemed...

I am self-esteemed!

self-es*teemed *adj.* having respect for or a favorable impression of oneself.

Be Sensitive

Open your heart and be in tune with how you feel.
Treat other people's feelings with similar care and respect.
However,
don't expect other people's sensitivities or sensibilities
to match up with your own...
you'd be setting yourself up for failure to do so.
It is personal prerogative
to touch, taste, sense and feel the way you do.

I am sensitive!

sen*si*tive *adj.* 1. endowed with sensation. 2. readily or excessively affected by external agencies or influences. 3. having acute mental or emotional sensibility; easily affected, pained, annoyed, etc. 4. pertaining to, or connected with, the senses or sensation.

Be Serendipitous

Seek that which is important to you
to allow for synchronous discoveries.
Give assent for things to come "out of the blue" for you.
Enjoy making unforeseen connections
and watch for signs pointing you toward feeling blissfull.
Life is a synchronicity dance.

I feel serendipitous...

I am serendipitous!

ser*en*dip*i*tous *adj.* experiencing the aptitude for making desirable discoveries by seeming accident.

Be Serene

Picture in your mind a calm, sky-reflecting lake.
Remain unruffled in the midst of the winds of human drama.
Take counsel in the peaceful
and feel yourself floating on a sea of tranquility.
Be fair and clear.
Enjoy Life and Light!

I feel serene...

I am serene!

se*rene *adj.* 1. calm, peaceful, or tranquil; unperturbed; composed. 2. clear; fair: *serene weather.* 3. most high or august, used as a royal epithet (*usually capitalized and preceded by his, her, your, etc.*): *his Serene Highness.* 4. focused.

Be Sharing

Life is easiest as a team.
Find someone to share rides with.
Pool your resources with those you know.
Participate for better and best, in healing and in life.
The benefits of having a partner are inherent in any relationship.
Pull a "Buffett" and add Billions... to Billions.

I feel like sharing...

I am sharing!

shar*ing *adj.* 1. acting as a part of a whole, especially as an assigned member of a group. 2. using, participating in, enjoying, receiving, etc. jointly: *The two chemists are sharing the Nobel prize.* 3. giving or receiving equally as a team. 4. partaking of something common in common. (*Ed. Note* "Buffett" refers to Warren E. Buffett)

Be Sharp

The art of introducing the future is yours for the making.
Be on the leading edge of life
and possess a mentally acute, alert and vigilant mind.
The steering wheel of life is in your hands.
Be a responsible driver.

I feel sharp...

I am sharp!

sharp *adj*. 1. having a thin cutting edge or a fine point; well-adapted for cutting or piercing: *a sharp knife*. 2. terminating in an edge or point; not blunt or rounded: *The table has sharp corners*. 3. clearly defined; distinct: *a sharper image; sharp differences of opinion*. 4. mentally acute, aware, or observant: *a sharp lad; a sharp watch for the enemy*. 5. very stylish: *a sharp dresser; a sharp jacket*.

Be Significant

Let the purpose of your life
contain a remarkable kind of presence and importance.
Who you feel and believe yourself to be
has consequences beyond belief.
The ripple from the pebble you throw in life's pond
is more than noteworthy.
Feel worthy of becoming a legend.

I feel significant...

I am significant!

sig*nif*i*cant *adj*. 1. important; of consequence. 2. having, or expressing, a meaning. 3. having a special, secret, or disguised meaning: *a significant wink*.

Be Sincere

Be genuine,
free from deceit and hypocrisy,
and enjoy the distinction of a deeply meaningful life.
Go below the surface
and find your connection to mind goes deeper still.
Confirm connection
with your source, your nature and your destiny.
Stand on your own two feet.

I feel sincere...

I am sincere!

sin*cere *adj.* 1. free from deceit, hypocrisy, or falseness; earnest: *a sincere letter of apology.* 2. genuine; unfeigned.

Be Skillful

Level Four: Unconscious Incompetence
Level Three: Conscious Incompetence
Level Two: Conscious Competence
Level One: Unconscious Competence
Enough said!

I am skillful!

skill*ful *adj.* 1. the ability to do something well, arising from talent, training, and/or practice: *her skillful art produced incredible beauty and plenty of money.*
2. competent excellence in performance. 3. understanding; discernment.

Be Smart

Work smart, not just hard.
Use leverage to move great weight and tool the mind for creation.
Think clearly and concisely
about matters of science and mathematics.
Observe what does work and what does not work.
Learn from mistakes and grow from experience.
Remember... to outfox the fox... think outside the FOX.

I'm smart... I feel smart.

smart *adj.* 1. having or showing quick intelligence or ready mental capabilities.
2. shrewd or sharp, as a person in dealing with others. 3. clever, witty, or readily
effective as a speaker, speech, rejoinder, etc. 4. dashingly or impressively neat or
trim in appearance, as a person or a garment. 5. socially elegant; sophisticated or
fashionable: *the smart crowd.*

Be Sociable

"Come out, come out!
Come out from your cocoon, oh sweet butterfly!"
Between us there is so much to learn
and, oh so much more to enjoy.
I've never had so much fun,
in my entire life, than being here with you.
I'm inclined to associate with those like you,
and am predisposed toward friendships with similar intentions.
"So! Let's make friends!"

I feel sociable...

I am sociable!

so*cia*ble *adj.* 1 inclined to associate with or be in the company of others.
2. friendly or agreeable in company; companionable. 3. disposed toward living in
companionship with others rather than in isolation: *Man is a sociable creature.*

Be Soulful

Draw upon the deepest parts of yourself,
and express the dance, art, music and literature of life
that dwell within the Akashic records of the mind.
Know your soul; touch the seeds of truth, beauty and goodness.
Feel the history of your life being written
as you inscribe your signature today...
within the pages of tomorrow.
Feel the Source of Life and Light within you!

I feel soulful...

I am soulful!

soul*ful *adj.* 1 of, or expressive of, deep feelings or emotions. 2. the animated
principle; the essential element or part of something. 3. the embodiment of
abstract quality.

Be Special

Be distinct in your personal characteristics.
Combine qualities of your choice... like no one else.
Give yourself permission to stand apart from others.
The price of blending in and becoming "normal"
is higher than being unique.

I feel special...

I am special!

spe*cial *adj.* 1. of a distinct or particular kind of character: *a special kind of key.*
2. having a particular function, purpose, application, etc.: *a special messenger.*
3. dealing with particulars; specific: *a special statement.*

Be Spectacular

Live life to the fullest.
First impressions have lasting effects.
Display yourself dramatically whenever you so desire
and let your adventures be so daring
as to accomplish the thrilling and brilliant.
Tales of your accomplishments are bigger than life
and prompt you to feel quite impressive.

I feel spectacular... I am spectacular...

I... am... spectacular!

spec*tac*u*lar *adj.* 1. of, or like, a spectacle; marked by, or given to, an impressive, large-scale display. 2. dramatically daring or thrilling.

Be Spiritual

The wind will blow where it will.
The rain will find its way back to the sea.
The most spiritual spirit of all is Love.
Embody the ideals of truth, beauty and goodness.

I am spiritual!

spir*it*u*al *adj.* 1. pertaining to, or consisting of, the incorporeal part of men and women in general, or of the individual, or an aspect of this, such as the mind or soul. 2. of, or pertaining to, the moods or feelings and like concerns, as distinguished from bodily or worldly existence or its concerns. 3. characterized by or suggesting predominance of the spirit or things of the supernatural. 4. collective participation of, and adoption of attitudes by, an elementary school as for team sports or departmental scholastics (*as opposed to religious superiority, national sovereignty or political beliefs.*)

Be Splendid

Go beyond the ordinary.
Exude a refined sense of sparkling beauty
and a remarkable presence of divine goodness.
Let your qualities be marvelous and strikingly admirable.
Adopt the attributes, aptitudes and attitudes of this book
and command them
to make you shine like the stars in the heavens.
Make these attitudes yours.
Own your splendor.

I feel splendid...

I am splendid!

spen*did *adj.* 1. magnificent or sumptuous. 2. grand or superb as beauty.
3. distinguished or glorious. 4. stunningly excellent or fine: *splendid talents.*

Be Spontaneous

Have a fabulous propensity
for expressing yourself in the moment.
Say what you feel needs to be said, when it needs to be said.
Go forward in everyday movement, ideas and relationships...
spontaneously.

When I feel like being spontaneous...

I'm... spontaneous!

spon*ta*ne*ous *adj.* 1. coming from, or resulting from, a natural impulse or tendency; without effort or premeditation. 2. (*of a person*) given to acting upon sudden
impulses. 3. (*of natural phenomena*) arising from internal forces or causes.

Be Stellar

Assume the position and posture of success.
Shine inside the bauble of your universe.
Glitter like a star within your field of endeavor.
Dwell on aspects and issues
that have potentially far reaching effects.
A spectacular life is yours for the asking
and taking within this universe!

I feel stellar...

I am stellar!

stel*lar *adj.* 1. of, or pertaining to, the stars; consisting of stars. 2. like a star, as in brilliance, shape, etc. 3. prominent in some field, as of entertainment or sports: *His stellar performance made his career.*

Be Still

Learn to feel the flow of time.
Grow past survival into the realm of simply "Being."
Maintain pace with this perspective.
Keep on... keeping on.

I am still!

still *adj.* 1. continuing at this or that time; as preciously: *Are you still here?* 2. up to this or that time; as yet. 3. in the future as in the past: *Modifications will still be made.*

Be Stimulating

Be a force to be reckoned with.
Incite effort with personal participation.
Rouse others to action with positive encouragement.
Act as a catalyst in helping people achieve great things.
The action of needing money is like kneading dough.
You must take action before you stop, take a rest and let it rise.

I feel stimulating...

I am stimulating!

stim*u*lat*ing *adj.* 1. something that quickens some vital process or functional
activity. 2. quickening some vital process or functional activity.

Be Striving

On the surface of today
etch your efforts into the crystal granite of time.
Like potters clay,
an unfulfilled destiny awaits the hands-on shaping of your will.
So, exert yourself vigorously
in applying your thoughts and feelings...
repetitively reaching for your dreams
'til you catch them and make them yours.

I feel like striving...

I am striving!

striv*ing *adj.* 1. making strenuous efforts toward any goal: to strive for success.
2. remaining motivated.

Be Strong

Deliver fabulous results through use
of great physical, mental and mechanical power.
Strength lays not so much in how it's used but in why it's used.
The true possessor of power
is the one who chooses not to lord it over others,
but, to use it to reveal the absolute strength
in the power and presence of the Source,
of the truth, beauty, and goodness within all.
Command a robust presence with both seen and unseen force.

I feel strong... (growled) waaa

I... am... strong!

strong *adj.* 1. able to exert great bodily or muscular power; physically vigorous or robust. 2. mentally powerful or vigorous: *Although very old... his mind is still strong.* 3. especially able, competent or powerful in a specific field of respect: *She's very strong in mathematics and perception by intuition.* 4. of great moral power, firmness, or courage. 5. powerful in influence, resources, or means of prevailing: *a strong nation.*

Be Studious

When studying,
take into account the nature of the source of the information
including the background and insight of the teacher.
Invest in your mind; investigate your environment
and acknowledge and appreciate your realities.
Examine and scrutinize
as many aspects as you can in your studies.
Be zealous in your analysis... Oh Great Observer!

I am studious!

stu*di*ous *adj.* 1. disposed or given to study: *a studious boy and girl.*
2. characterized by study or a disposition to study: *studious tasks.* 3. zealous, assiduous, or painstaking: *studious care.*

Be Stupendous

Accomplish what only dreamers can imagine:
awesome results and wondrous experiences.
Undertake that which is out of this world
and has never been before.
Express a marvelous presence
with who and what you believe you are.
Be splendid, breathtaking and fantastic.

I feel stupendous... I am stupendous!

stu*pen*dous *adj.* 1. causing amazement; astounding, marvelous: *stupendous news.* 2. amazingly large or great; immense; prodigious: *their athletic achievements were stupendous.*

Be Subjective

Objectivity is form, whereas subjectivity is content.
Glue your relationships together with a healthy balance of each.
Engage personality before employing impersonality.
Intuition leads to understanding, which builds knowledge,
which in turn holds counsel to fortify courage
for envisioning and acting toward
the wisest of potential outcomes.
The object of one thing often leads to the subject of another.

I feel subjective... I am subjective!

sub*jec*tive *adj.* 1. existing in the mind; belonging to the thinking subject rather than to the object of thought (*as opposed to objective*). 2. pertaining to, or on the part of, an individual; personal; individual: *a subjective evaluation.* 3. placing emphasis or reliance on one's own moods, attitudes, opinions, etc. 4. relating to, or of the nature of, an object as it is known in the mind as distinct from the thought of a thing in itself.

164

Be Substantial

Let there be merit in your accomplishments,
and boost the effects of your life in revealing true value.
Weigh meanings in terms with what you know and understand.
Instill worth in things that matter and mean something to you,
as well as other subjects that spark inspiration for a fuller life.

I feel substantial...

I am substantial!

sub*stan*tial *adj.* 1. of ample or considerable amount, quantity, size, etc.: *the armored truck had substantial room for the cash.* 2. of solid character or quality; essential; fundamental. 3. wealthy or influential. 4. of real worth, value, or effect: *substantial reasons.*

Be Subtle

Be cleverly skillful, skillfully clever and ingenious.
Possess a quiet demeanor
and magnetically attract trustworthy characters.
Be tacitly delicate when mentioning private matters.
Deliver results, which require mental acuteness and mystery.
Speak the truth and let they who have ears to hear, listen.

I feel subtle...

I am subtle!

sub*tle *adj.* 1. thin, tenuous, or rarefied, as a fluid or an odor. 2. fine or delicate in meaning or intent; difficult to perceive or understand: *subtle irony.* 3. delicate or faint and mysterious: *a subtle smile; a subtle glance.* 4. characterized by or requiring mental acuteness, penetration or discernment: *a subtle understanding; a subtle philosophy.*

Be Successful

Turn mistakes, bad news, failures and disappointments
into the stepping-stones toward success.
Let this success bring the next success,
and then the next and so forth.
Attend to your life with feelings of appreciation
for achievement and attainment.
Enjoy your rewards, prizes, honors and compliments.
Acknowledge the accomplishments you've already achieved.
Know what its like to be entirely satisfied.

I feel successful...

I am successful!

suc*cess*ful *adj.* 1. achieving or having achieved success in performance: *Her practice is successful.* 2. having attained wealth, position, honors, or the like. 3. resulting in, or attended with, the favorable or prosperous termination of attempts; fruitful endeavors.

Be Sunny

Reflect the brightness of a happy outlook.
Applaud that which is joyous and cheerful...
like blue sky on an afternoon day.
Emote rays of joy and feelings of happiness
in spite of the shadow of darkness and closure of doors.
Remember, the darker things seem to get
means the light nearby is shinning even more brightly.
Become a source of illumination for others;
reflect the Source of Life and Light.

I feel sunny...

I am sunny!

sun*ny *adj.* 1. abounding in cheeriness or happiness. 2. pleasant and hopeful.

Be Supportive

Assist others, giving aid as part of a team.
Act to provide stability for your partner's attitude.
Encourage their positive participation
by supplying a loving approach to them in your communication.
Show them they're appreciated by the feedback you offer.
The more you have, the more you can give, if you so choose.
"Give a man a fish and you feed him for a day.
Teach his children to fish
and you feed his community for a long time."

I feel supportive...
I am supportive!

sup*port*ive *adj.* 1. providing support: *She was supportive of his new position with the company.* 2. maintaining that which serves as a foundation. 3. to sustain or withstand (*weight, pressure, stress, strain, time etc.*). 4. to sustain (*a person, their spirit, etc.*) under perceived affliction.

Be Sure

Let your mind attain a level of faith
which is free from doubt
as to reliability, character and action of the universe.
Re-examine your core beliefs
and proceed feeling confident in what to expect.
Learn to balance uncertainty...
as the original author of certainty.
Be sublime in the face of the unknown.

I feel sure... I'm sure!

sure *adj.* 1. free from doubt as to the reliability, character, action, etc. of something (*often followed by of*): to be sure of one's facts. 2. confident, as of something expected. 3. convinced, fully persuaded, or positive. 4. assured or certain beyond question: *His death is sure.* 5. worthy of confidence; reliable; stable. 6. unfailing: *a sure cure.* 7. destined; bound inevitably; certain.

Be Swell

Be a buddy for someone.
Know that your influence would be timely and vital.
Let your musing be the cat's meow
or the dogs bow-wow for one of your friends.
Allow serendipity and synchronicity between you and your mate.
When it's their turn to talk, listen to them
and respond without turning it into or making it about you!

I feel swell...

I am swell!

swell *adj.* 1. (*of things*) stylish; elegant: *a swell hotel.* 2. (*of persons*) fashionably
dressed or socially prominent: *a swell friend.* 3. first rate; fine.

Be Swift

When the time comes – be capable of moving with great speed.
Respond quickly to opportunity.
When the universe gives you an answer to your request
recognize it and move readily in sequence.
Seek to be first-rate when delivering requests and quotes
and proficient in receiving answers and fulfilling orders.
Be happening.

I feel swift...

I am swift!

swift *adj.* 1. moving or capable of moving with great speed. 2. coming, happening,
or performing quickly. 3. quick to act or respond. 4. sensitive to intuition.

Be Synergistic

Let one plus one equal three.
Work together to endorse a sum greater than its parts.
A three-sided structure is the strongest foundation
in our known universe.
Blend with others of like mind
and watch the honey-pot get richer and fuller.

I am synergistic!

syn*er*gis*tic *adj.* 1. the joint action of agents, as drugs, that when taken together increases each other's effectiveness. 2. a body organ, medicine, effort, etc. that cooperates with another or others to produce or enhance an effect: *His physical healing and mental recuperation efforts were synergistic.* 3. combined action.

Be Talented

Take out your talents and polish them with practice.
Discover what your talents are
by finding out what makes you happy.
You will discover that your talents are unique to you.
Find a coach to make the best of those talents
and take delight in performing or playing.

I am talented.

I feel talented.

tal*ent*ed *adj.* 1. having a special natural ability or aptitude: *a talent for drawing.* 2. containing a capacity for achievement or success; ability: *younger and older men and women of talent.* 3. inclination or disposition.

Be Tactful

Be diplomatic in your dealings with others.
Exercise discreet sensitivity
with passing events and sharing information.
Manifest a keen sense of what to do or say
to avoid offending others.
Learn how to instruct others on what to do,
such that they look forward to doing it.

I am tactful!

tact*ful *adj.* having or manifesting a sharp feeling or sense for what is appropriate, tasteful, or aesthetically pleasing.

Be Teachable

Be capable of being taught by being open to instruction.
Increase your net worth through guidance, training and practice.
There is always room for improvement,
so what are you waiting for?
Let your teacher edify what you need to know
and coach you into position for performance.

I feel I'm teachable...

I am teachable!

teach*a*ble *adj.* 1. capable of being instructed, as a person. 2. absorb knowledge of, or skill in.

Be Tenacious

Hold fast to your beliefs.
Train your mind to be highly retentive.
Program your personality software
with an assiduous sense for detail.
Have the uncanny ability to persevere
in the midst of trials and tribulations.
Extricate yourself from the most difficult of situations
with all due alacrity.

I am tenacious!

te*na*cious *adj.* 1. characterized by keeping a firm hold (*often followed by of*):
a tenacious grip on my arm; tenacious of old habits. 2. highly retentive:
a tenacious memory. 3. holding together; cohesive; not easily pulled asunder.

Be Tender

When you caress...
do so with a soft touch and a warm demeanor.
Move easily within personal empathy and compassion.
Use insight and perception of the here and now
to prepare time and space for Love.
Be gentle, sensitive and expressive
in caring for someone with affection.

I feel tender...

I am tender!

ten*der *adj.* 1. soft or delicate in substance; not hard or tough: *a tender steak.*
2. affectionate or loving; sentimental or amatory: *a tender glance.*

Be Thankful

Feel appreciative and acknowledge pleasure in receiving
even with or without the desire or ability to respond in like kind.
Admit feelings of appreciation to strengthen the spirit
and express gratitude.
Optimistically encourage personal,
affirmative responses when called for.
Let positive reception edify spiritual observation.

I feel thankful...

I am thankful!

thank*ful *adj.* 1. feeling or expressing gratitude or appreciation. 2. verbalize insight
in realizing the worth of something. 3. observing receipt of gifts, honors and/or life.

Be Thinking

The element of a thought is a picture,
a moment frozen in time,
and the series of those elements... results in thinking.
How you feel about what you think about
determines your capacity to either attract or repel,
magnify or minimize that which you think about.
Let the river of thought fill your mind, offering a rationale to life
and liberate your spirit with feelings of great joy.
Design your thoughts
from the ideals you adopt, discover and develop.
Ponder your conjectures carefully because,
"To think is to create."
What are you creating?

I'm thinking!

think*ing *adj.* 1. to have a conscious mind, to some extent capable of reasoning, remembering experiences, making rational decisions, etc. 2. to employ one's mind rationally and objectively in evaluating or dealing with any given situation. 3. to have a certain thing as the subject of one's thought (*usually followed by of or about*). 4. to call something to one's conscious mind (*usually followed by of or about*). 5. to consider something as a possible action, choice, etc. (*usually followed by of*): *I'm thinking of going in that direction.* 6. to invent or conceive of something (*usually followed by of*). 7. to have consideration, or regard, for someone (*usually followed by of*). 8. to esteem a person or thing as indicated (*usually followed by of*): *to think well of someone; to think badly of someone.* 9. designing a plan or intention: *thinking of a way to move from here to there.*

Be Thoughtful

Be given toward handling images of Life and Light
with consideration for others, as well as for yourself.
Be mindful of the explosive nature of your contemplations.
It is better for your thinking
to be filled with thoughts that produce positive feelings
than negatives ones.
Remember, "To think is to create."
To feel is to Know!

I am thoughtful!

thought*ful *adj.* 1. occupied with or given to thought; contemplative; meditative; reflective: *in a thoughtful mood.* 2. characterized by, or manifesting, careful thought: *a thoughtful essay.* 3. careful, heedful; mindful: *to be thoughtful of one's safety.* 4. showing consideration for others; considerate.

Be Thrifty

Participate in the world of economics.
Learn how to manage your personal economy.
Make the most of your money.
Make the most of your talents.
Make the most of your energy.
Make the most of your time.
Make the most of your mind.
Make the most of your feelings...

I feel thrifty...

I am thrifty!

thrift*y *adj.* 1. practicing economical management; economy: *the company was well-run by thrifty employees.* 2. frugality: *a thrifty housewife.*

Be Timeless

Restrict yourself to no particular time.
Be part of the past as well as of the future.
Time-travel by means of consequential thinking.
A myriad of time-lines are possible
and selected or adopted by you in the here and now.

I feel timeless...

I am timeless!

time*less *adj.* 1. without beginning or end; eternal; everlasting. 2. referring or restricted to no particular time: *the timeless beauty of great music.*

Be Tolerant

Support others, as you would yourself wish to be supported.
Be able to withstand disappointment, depression and dismissal.
Allow others time to make space... and space to make time.
Pardon inconveniencies with patience and understanding.
Choose a new attitude daily
and cultivate days filled with gratitude.
Have a predisposition toward endurance.

I feel tolerant...

I am tolerant!

tol*er*ant *adj.* 1. allowing without prohibition or hindrance; permitting. 2. enduring without repugnance; to put up with: *I can tolerate laziness, but not sloth.*
3. to endure or resist the action of a drug, poison, prison, etc. 4. to experience, undergo, or sustain pain or hardship: *they were tolerant of boot camp.*

Be Tough

Be able to withstand hardships.
Be resistant toward the mental and physical viruses,
which are ever present.
Feel sturdy in your walk and steadfast in your journey.
Be tenacious and let nothing disturb your peace of mind.
Be poised for serenity.

I feel tough...

I am tough!

tough *adj.* 1. strong and durable; not easily broken or cut. 2. not brittle or tender.
3. capable of great endurance; sturdy; hardy: *tough troops.*

Be Tranquil

Be free from long lasting effects of disturbing emotions.
Feel liberated from commotion and tumultuous conditions.
Enjoy happiness and find comfort;
feel like an island paradise in a sea of tranquility.
Observe balance within your perspective: you can do it, relax.

I feel tranquil...

I am tranquil!

tran*quil *adj.* 1. free from commotion or tumult; peaceful; quiet; calm: *a tranquil country place.* 2. free from, or unaffected by, disturbing emotions; unagitated; serene; placid: *a tranquil life.*

Be Transcendental

Surpass your expected station in life
and clothe yourself with that which you feel you can become.
Go beyond ordinary boundary limitations.
Rise to the occasion of being you
and move into new territory, a new personality.
Your eternal, internal ascension career awaits you.

I am transcendental!

tran*scen*den*tal *adj.* 1. transcendent, surpassing, or superior. 2. being beyond ordinary or common experience, thought, or belief; supernatural. 3. abstract or metaphysical.

Be Triumphant

Try with oomph.
Rejoice over victorious accomplishment.
Feel ever so exultant within the magnificence of life,
achieving success, health and justice.
Enjoy your trophies.

I am triumphant!

I feel GREAT!

tri*um*phant *adj.* 1. having achieved victory or success; victorious; successful.
2. exulting over victory; rejoicing over success; exultant.

Be True

Represent the truth.
Remain honest and loyal to your word.
Feel faithful to the authentic...
in the best and most desirable sense.
Reflect sincerely upon the truth
as your feelings and considerations
agree to the intentions of fact, action and decision.

I am true!

true *adj.* 1. in accordance with, or not contrary to, fact. 2. having a basis in fact:
not fiction, but a true story. 3. being really such; authentic: *true vanilla flavoring.*
4. being such in the best or most desirable sense: *true statesmanship.* 5. loyal;
faithful. 6. reflecting sincerely one's feelings or intentions: *true amusement.*
7. exact; accurate; of the proper form: *a true copy; a true surface.*

Be Trustworthy

Generate belief in you... by others
for your dependability and reliability
by creating assurance of this in yourself first.
Being worthy of trust is not to be given over to lightly;
it must be earned.
Being trustworthy is a side effect
of aligning yourself with the truth of honesty.

I feel trustworthy...

I am trustworthy!

trust*wor*thy *adj.* 1. deserving of trust or confidence; dependable; reliable.
2. reliable in integrity, ability, surety, etc. of a person or thing. 3. expected
confidence of something; hoped for.

Be Tuned In

Become frequency specific
toward that which you feel you want or wish for.
Either be entertained by the station you choose
or change the channel.
Acceptance of situations
and appreciation of conditions reflect your choices.
Become acquainted
with the potential possibilities available to you.

I feel tuned in...

I am... tuned in!

tuned * in *adj.* 1. to adjust (*a motor, mechanism, or the like*) for proper functioning.
2. to adjust a receiving apparatus so as to receive (*the signals of a particular
transmitting station*). 3. to put into or cause to be in a receptive condition, mood, etc.

Be Unafraid

Fear need not impair you.
F.E.A.R. is False Evidence Appearing Real.
Use fear to bring attention to matters needing awareness.
And, grief need not immobilize you: embrace it and then let it go!
Move through feelings of discomfort,
betrayal and disappointment
with a state of mind that allows
for reversion to personal serenity and peace .
You are not alone within the realm of the "I Am!"

I feel unafraid...

I am... unafraid!

un*a*fraid *adj.* 1. without fear. 2. already convinced.

Be Unconditional

Live your life with whole-hearted participation
without endlessly pre-qualifying necessities before doing so.
Let the sinews of your integrity
and the ligaments of your sincerity
support the muscles of your intentions.
Act positively and without reservation.
Be part of this eternal river of ever-changing time and space.

I feel unconditional...

I am unconditional!

un*con*di*tion*al *adj.* not limited by conditions; unqualified absolute.

Be Undaunted

Hold onto your visions firmly and clearly.
Fuel imagination with insipid inspiration of courage in daily life
and imaginings of valor in stories that echo through time.
Feel yourself move solidly toward your goal posts.
Keep your eyes on the prize; don't pay attention to anything less.
If it's cost you this much... to go this far... in this direction...
it'll cost just as much or more to go back the other way.

I feel undaunted...

I am undaunted!

un*daunt*ed *adj.* 1. undismayed; not discouraged; not forced to abandon purpose or effort. 2. undiminished in courage or valor; not giving way to fear; intrepid.

Be Understanding

Demonstrate your ability to interpret information.
Engage your mind with reason, common sense
and concepts which act to scaffold
your awareness, knowledge and appreciation.
Observe the association of differing ideas
and relegate varying perceptions.
Comprehend the meaning
of what's being said and what's not being said.

I'm understanding!

un*der*stand*ing *adj.* 1. perceiving the meaning of; grasping the idea of; comprehending: *understanding Spanish, French or any of the other 8000 exotic languages.* 2. to be thoroughly familiar with; apprehending clearly the character, nature, or subtleties of: *understanding a trade; understanding a poem.* 3. assigning a meaning to; interpreting: *He is incorrectly understanding her suggestion as a complaint.* 4. grasping the significance of, or importance of. 5. perceiving what is meant; grasping the information conveyed.

Be Unique

Be incomparable.
Cast your shadow.
Stand alone in your particular qualities.
Adopt the attributes of the adventuring avatar.
Apply your own distinct characteristics as to who you are,
what you do and how you do it.

I feel unique...

I am unique!

u*nique *adj.* 1. existing as the only one or as the sole example; single; solitary
in type or characteristics. 2. having no like or equal; standing alone in quality;
incomparable: *She succeeded because she was unique.*

Be Unlimited

Nothing is beyond you.
Modify both thinking and feeling
to include that which is boundless, infinite and vast
within your sphere of existence.
Adjust your "real eyes" to see the unlimited potential
and infinite possibilities that exist.
Drink a glass of water and touch the endless river.

I feel unlimited...

I am unlimited!

un*lim*it*ed *adj.* 1. without limitations or restrictions. 2. boundless; limitless;
infinite; vast. 3. without any qualification or exception: *unlimited surrender.*

Be Unpredictable

Ok! Except in one area!
Always move toward the positive.
Avoid falling into a rut (a grave with its ends knocked out)
by always moving toward the unqualified absolute.
Seek to qualify not just quantify your life.
If you want something you've never had before
you must be willing to do what you've never done before.
Create and recreate.

I feel unpredictable...

I am unpredictable!

un*pre*dict*a*ble *adj.* 1. not predictable; not to be foreseen or foretold.
2. preverbal. 3. not always the same. 4. not boring.

Be Unusual

Choose to be "exceptional" in character,
not necessarily "normal."
Develop personality traits,
which richly include that, which is uncommon.
Don't be "bore denary."
Erm... I mean... don't be ordinary!

I'm unusual!

un*u*su*al *adj.* not usual, common, or ordinary; uncommon in amount or degree;
exceptional. (*Ed. Note:* 1. denary means pertaining to that, which is a squalid, den
like concept or stance of perception, whereas; 2. bore means to be a source of
petty annoyance as a dull tiresome person: *hence a bore denary outcome.*)

Be Valiant

In the face of adversity
enlist courageous approaches and valorous attitudes.
Defend worthiness with excellence in consideration and action.
Stand boldly on principal rather than popularity.
If you live in a kingdom, represent the king and queen.
If you live in a republic, represent the people.
If you live in today's society, represent the family.
If you live in the presence of god, represent God.
Represent the best of all mythologolites.

I feel valiant...

I am valiant!

val*iant *adj.* 1. boldly spirited; brave; stout-hearted: *a valiant soldier.* 2. marked by or showing bravery or valor; heroic. 3. worthy; excellent. *(Ed. Note.* mythologolites is a word used to describe inherited schools of family.)

Be Versatile

Be capable of turning easily from one task to another:
cleverly adaptable.
Let your skills have many applications.
For every field of expertise there are side-fields.
Be acquainted and adept with these side-fields as well.
Manipulate multiple missions.

I am versatile!

I feel versatile!

ver*sa*tile *adj.* 1. able to move from one task to another. 2. near the middle so as to be able to turn from event to event, situation to situation, or project to project, easily.

Be Vibrant

Vibrancy is the feeling that charges the magnet of your mind.
Exude excitement in your personality.
Affect others with self-assured energy.
Shimmer with vitality.
Feel electrified.

I feel ... vibrant.

I am vibrant!

vi*brant *adj.* 1. moving to and from rapidly; vibrating. 2. (*of sounds*) characterized by perceptible vibration; resonic, resonant; resounding: *the speaker cone is vibrant.* 3. pulsating with vigor and energy. 4. exciting or stimulating; lively: *she walked onto the stage with a vibrant sway.*

Be Vigilant

Maintain a careful observance for safety.
Be mindful and take action
to protect what you consider valuable.
Act as a vanguard for your mind
and let in only those thoughts that are worthy of you.
Be the gatekeeper
for those who would enter either your mind or your life.

I am vigilant!

vig*i*lant *adj.* 1. keenly watchful to detect danger or trouble. 2. ever awake and alert; sleeplessly watchful.

Be Vigorous

Choose to feel robust in your efforts.
Touch your world with emotion and move with energy to spare.
Saturate your character with energetic vim and vitality.
Command your body, mind, spirit and universe
with a childlike enthusiasm.

I feel vigorous...

I am vigorous!

vig*or*ous *adj.* 1. full of or characterized by vigor: a vigorous effort. 2. strong or
active; robust. 3. energetic; forceful.

Be Virtuous

Represent the best in human nature.
Produce effects resulting from efforts of pure motivations,
modest assumptions and even-temperaments.
Be morally excellent and chaste in your ethical principles.
Become acquainted with the virtues you possess
and showcase them in your life.

I feel virtuous...

I am virtuous!

vir*tu*ous *adj.* 1. conforming to moral and ethical principles; morally excellent;
upright. 2. chaste, as a person. 3. principia.

Be Vivacious

Be lively in your movements and animated in physical action.
Exuberate the essence of Life and Light.
Sing your song.
Hum your ditty!
Feel your presence of mind
rejuvenate those around you.
Repeat: "I am the light of my world."
Be analogous to the wind on a gusty day.

I feel vivacious...

I am vivacious!

vi*va*cious *adj.* 1. lively or animated; sprightly. 2. long-lived, or tenacious of life.

Be Vivid

Breathe deeply the gathering freshness of life into yourself
and, hence, into those around you.
Shimmer with exciting colors and a compelling presence.
It's the sizzle, taste and aroma,
not the steak itself, that sells like hotcakes.
The power of an idea lies not so much in how certain or valid it is
but how vividly it appears.

I feel vivid...

I am vivid!

viv*id *adj.* 1. strikingly bright or intense, as color or light. 2. full of life; lively; animated: *a vivid personality.* 3. presenting the appearance, freshness, spirit, etc., of life: *a vivid painting; a vivid street scene.* 4. strong, distinct, or clearly perceptible: *a vivid impression.* 5. forming distinct and striking mental imagery: *a vivid imagination.*

186

Be Warm

Enrich your daily journey with a friendly disposition.
Act kindly toward those you meet.
Share lively feelings with sincere emotions.
Be affectionate and demonstrate a warm friendship of love.

I feel warm...

I am warm!

warm *adj.* 1. friendly, kindly, or affectionate. 2. characterized by, or showing, lively feelings, emotions, etc.: *warm interest*. 3. lively or vigorous: *a warm debate*. 4. strong or fresh: *a warm scent*.

Be Wealthy

Take a look at your life and acknowledge the abundance therein.
Dwell on the positive side of the Bridge Over Wishing River.
You have so much to be grateful for.
From riches take riches... and still riches remain.
Give thanks and admit victory over the material world.
Those who believe they have... will more be given.
You were designed to live an abundant life.

I feel wealthy...

I am wealthy.

wealth*y *adj.* 1. having great wealth; rich; affluent. 2. having any stated or implied thing in great abundance. (*Ed. Note.* Discover the Bridge over Wishing River at www.bebe.bz)

Be Welcome

You are welcome.
This is the final response from enjoying the creative process.
This expresses gratitude
and deep appreciation for what's been asked for.
Take the time to get to know this attitude of gratitude.

I feel welcome...

I am welcome.

You... are welcome.

wel*come *verb.* a greeting as to a person whose arrival gives pleasure: *Welcome stranger.* - *noun..* a kindly greeting or reception: to give someone a warm welcome. - *verb transitive.* 1. to greet the arrival of (*a person, guests, etc.*) with pleasure or kindly courtesy. 2. to accept with pleasure.

Be Well

Experience your body
as being in a constant state of healing itself.
Thrive wholeheartedly within the present Kingdom of Being...
The Garden of Isdom!
Center yourself
in the midst of all that is true, beautiful and good,
holy, just and great!
Feel happy and contented with the way things are...
and the way things are becoming.

I feel well... I am well!

well *adj.* 1. in a good or satisfactory manner: *things are well.* 2. in a careful or thorough manner: listen well: *shake well before using.* 3. in a moral or proper manner: *to behave well.* 4. commendably, meritoriously, or excellently: *a difficult task done well.* 5. with propriety, justice, or reason: *I could not well refuse.* 6. favorably: *to think well of someone.*

Be Well-Balanced

Neither be too far right nor too far left
in your politics, religions, and other ideologies and be-ologies.
Seek to exist in a state of equilibrium
within your sphere of existence.
Make necessary adjustments to maintain balance.
Observe how both cause and effect apply respective influence.

I feel well balanced...

I am well balanced!

well-bal*anced *adj.* 1. rightly balanced, adjusted, or regulated: *a well-balanced diet.* 2. sensible; sane: *a well-balanced mind.*

Be Well-Read

Expose yourself to the thoughts and feelings of others.
Build a personal knowledge bank
through the efforts of voracious reading.
Develop the library that is your imagination
and educate your mind.
Read as much as you can.
Don't just wait to watch the movie.

I am well-read!

well-read *adj.* 1. well-informed through reading. 2. having acquired knowledge or enlightenment through books, magazines, mass media, contents of libraries as well as Akashic Mind records: *he won $250,000,000 playing Jeopardy® because he was well-read!*

Be Well-Rounded

Pursue varied abilities and actual attainments.
Become fully developed
and maintain balance in your personality.
Animate the best features in your balanced personal presence.
Know something about widely different things.

I feel well rounded...

I am well rounded!

well-round*ed *adj.* 1. having desirably varied abilities or attainments. 2. desirably varied: *a well-rounded curriculum.*

Be Well-Spoken

If your foot slips, you can recover from your fall.
If your tongue slips, you may never recover at all.
Express yourself carefully and with knowledgeable intent.
Others will remember you for what you've said
and how you said it.

I am well-spoken!

well-spo*ken *adj.* 1. speaking well, fittingly, or pleasingly: *The new chairwoman was very well-spoken.* 2. spoken in an apt, fitting, or pleasing manner: *a few well-spoken words on civic pride.*

Be Willing

Design your wishes and desires
according to what you dream about.
Deliberately choose actions based upon intelligent reflection.
The concept of free will rests upon your willingness to be willing.
With courage, agree to be ready
to participate in the dignity of free will.

I feel willing...

I am willing!

will*ing *adj.* 1. disposed or consenting; inclined: *I am willing to go despite their attitude.* 2. cheerfully consenting or ready: *He is a willing worker.* 3. done, given, borne, used, etc., with cheerful readiness: *They were willing to live in peace.*

Be Win-Win

Participate for results that are mutual in reward.
Prefer games and diversions
where the goals and aims are reciprocal.
Even in the win-lose world everyone still matters
because you can't even have a winner
without there being a loser. Both matter.
Be of the mind-set
that simply being part of the game makes you a winner.

I am win-win!

win-win *adj.* 1. taking part in games that are formatted so all participants are recognized as being the winner. 2. winning without lording that status over others. 3. to give as you have been given to. 4. to appreciate the goodness of victory for its own sake. 5. winners and co-winners (*as opposed to winners and losers.*)

Be Wise

Know that which is known to others and more.
Exercise the power of discernment,
reading between the lines with good judgment.
When intuition tells you something,
listen and adjust, act or react accordingly.
Choose with insight what you do today
in order to create the world you end up with tomorrow.

I feel wise... I am wise!

wise *adj.* 1. having the power of discerning and judging properly as to what is true or right; possessing discernment, judgment, or discretion. 2. characterized by or showing such power: *a wise decision.* 3. possessed of, or characterized by, scholarly knowledge or learning; learned; erudite: *wise in the law.* 4. in the know: *With her ear to the ground she became wise.*

Be Wishful

Imagine what it's like to do or to have what you've so longed for.
Contemplate your dreams as you select them with feeling
from this Catalog of Life and Light.
Aspire to ascend the ever inward, upward circles of attainment.
Light your wishes on fire and turn them into desires
with the soft whispering stories of inner voices.
Whisper, "Yes!" to yourself
as you select your dreams and ascribe perfection to yourself.

I am wishful!

wish*ful *adj.* 1. having or showing a wish; desirous. 2. feeling an impulse toward attainment or possession of something; to want, desire, or long for (*usually followed by an infinitive or a clause*): *I wish to travel. I wish that it were morning.* 3. desiring (*a person or thing*) to be (*as specified*): *to wish the problem settled.* 4. to bid, as in greeting or leave-taking: *to wish one a good morning; I wish you good day!* 5. to be full of wishes. 6. desirous of being or becoming perfect.

Be With-It

Traffic is no place to be independent.
Fly like birds in a flock
or swim like fish in a school, move "with" others in travel.
Be so intuit
that you're on the leading edge of your experience... of existence.
Get "with" the program
and make it something it couldn't have been
without your positive, practical participation.
So... get on with living your life.
It's so worthwhile.

I feel I'm with-it..."

I'm... with-it!

with*it *adj.* 1. accompanied by; connected: *He got the job because he was with-it.*
2. showing up; fully awake, aware, and perceptive. 3. inscrutably perfect: *Donald Trump couldn't fire them... because they were so with-it.*

Be Witty

Possess ingenuity in speech and writing.
Be amused with bright, intelligent insights.
Refine your sense of humor
to fit in with today's popular trends and trendsetters.
Permit your understanding
to be amusingly clever in perception and expression.

I am witty!

wit*ty *adj.* 1. possessing wit in acting, speech or writing; amusingly clever in perception and expression. 2. characterized by wit: *a witty remark.* 3. intelligent; clever: *Well, he wouldn't have to claim to be witty, if he were truly witty.*

Be You

Your identity is made up
with your memory, understanding and insight,
from what you remember, consider and imagine.
Become acquainted
with your Source, your nature and your destiny.
There is only one of you and without you...
the rest of us would not be complete.
You are the "I Am" within you.
I am the "I Am" within me.

I am you!

But...I feel like me!

you *adj.* 1. the pronoun of the second person singular or plural: *Did you do that? What happened to you? Did it help you?* 2. one; anyone; people in general: *a tiny animal you can't even see.* 3. your normal or customary self.

Be Youthful

Embrace a wholesome enjoyment of freshness and vigor.
Enliven your day
with the eternal qualities of innocence, curiosity and vitality.
Express happiness in play and possess a sense of living in peace.
Energize your activities daily with animated inquisitiveness.
Impress your playmates with amusing tales
and creative takes on words, meanings and feelings.

I feel youthful...

I am youthful!

youth*ful *adj.* 1. characterized by the condition of being young. 2. the vitality characteristic of having the appearance, freshness, vigor, or other qualities of youth and spring time. 3. being caught unaware of naïveté: *her youthful façade showed up on television.*

Be Zany

Emphasize your personality with dramatic humor.
Add a sense of fun to your self-image, and at times,
seek to surprise others with an unexpectedly good nature.
There's a time to be kooky and a time to be loopy,
... and a time to be neither.
Expertly discern which time is which, and when.

As I feel like being zany...

I am zany!

za*ny *adj.* 1. ludicrously or whimsically comical. 2. clownishly crazy: *leaving the theater they acted zany.* 3. a fun, silly person.

Be Zealous

Express your passions
and devote your intelligent feelings to diligent efforts.
Enthusiastically wish yourself and others
success in all endeavors.
Dream your desires come to pass, be these desires worthy of you!
Fervently work toward goals... inspired by plans you've designed.

I feel zealous...

I am zealous!

zeal*ous. *adj.* 1. full of, characterized by zeal. 2. resulting from fervor for a person, cause, or object; eagerly desiring or endeavoring. 3. ardently active, devoted, or enthusiastically diligent: *She was zealous for their dreams.*

Be Zesty

Overcome indolence and lethargy
by drawing a deep breath through your nose
holding it in at length...
and then blowing out hard, through tightly pursed lips.
Repeat this several times and energize your zeal for living.
Learn how to breath like a dolphin,
by coasting on the inhale side of respiration.
Spice your awareness with the oxygen required
for possibilities inherent in everyday living.
Zap your zing with an inhale here and zang a zesty exhale there.

I feel zesty...

I am zesty!

zest*y *adj.* 1. keenly relishing; heartily enjoying: *Your girlfriend is certainly zesty
tonight.* 2. full of gusto. 3. an agreeably tasty flavor imparted to something.
4. interesting; charming: *this sauce is a zesty addition to the party.*

I Be I

"Verbitudes to help make up your mind!"

By BeBe

The following are the most positive verbs in the English language, alphabetically arranged to spark your imagination, enrich your appreciation of Life and Light and create an incredible future!

Command these intentions with deliberatation and engage these actions available to you at any given time, place, event, or state, by modifying your ability and agility in selecting and utilizing each for becoming a better you.

This list contains over 1300 verbs from the English dictionary, a medium from which our collective culture creates our reality – always available to you, i.e. the (divine) Observer of Your life!

- A -
I abide
I abound
I accede
I accelerate
I accept
I access
I acclaim
I acclimate
I accommodate
I accompany
I accomplish
I accrue
I accumulate
I achieve
I acknowledge
I acquire
I act
I activate
I actualize
I adapt
I add
I adhere
I adjectify
I adjust
I administer
I administrate
I admire
I admit
I adopt
I adore
I adorn
I advance
I advertise
I advise
I advocate

I affect
I affirm
I agree
I aim
I allow
I allure
I am
I amend
I analyze
I anchor
I animate
I answer
I anticipate
I appear
I appease
I apply
I appraise
I appreciate
I approach
I appropriate
I approve
I arise
I arouse
I arrive
I articulate
I ascend
I ascertain
I ask
I aspirate
I assemble
I assert
I assimilate
I assist
I associate
I assure
I attain

I attempt
I attend
I attest
I attract
I attribute
I audit
I augment
I authorize
I award

- B -
I balance
I bathe
I be
I beam
I beatify
I beautify
I become
I begin
I behave
I behold
I believe
I belong
I benefit
I bequeath
I bestow
I blend
I bless
I blog
I bloom
I bounce-back
I breathe
I brew
I brighten
I bring
I build

- C -

I calculate
I calibrate
I call
I call-forth
I can
I captivate
I care
I caress
I carpe diem
I carry
I catalog
I catch
I categorize
I cause
I celebrate
I certify
I champion
I change
I channel
I chant
I characterize
I charge
I charm
I check
I cheer
I cherish
I chew
I choose
I circulate
I claim
I clarify
I clean
I climb
I clothe
I clown

I coach
I coax
I cogitate
I cognize
I collect
I color
I comb
I combine
I come
I comfort
I commend
I comment
I commit
I commune
I communicate
I compare
I compensate
I compete
I complement
I complete
I compliment
I comply
I compose
I comprehend
I compute
I conceive
I concentrate
I conceptualize
I conciliate
I conclude
I concur
I conduct
I confabulate
I confide
I confirm

I congratulate
I conjecture
I conjugate
I connect
I consent
I conserve
I consider
I console
I construct
I consult
I consume
I contact
I contain
I contemplate
I continue
I contribute
I control
I converse
I convey
I convince
I cook
I cooperate
I coordinate
I cope
I correct
I correspond
I corroborate
I could
I counsel
I count
I counterpoise
I couple
I course
I court
I cover
I craft

I crave
I create
I cultivate
I cure
I cycle

- D -
I dance
I dare
I daresay
I date
I daydream
I dazzle
I deal
I decide
I declare
I decorate
I dedicate
I deed
I defend
I define
I delegate
I deliberate
I delight
I deliver
I delve
I demand
I demonstrate
I denominate
I denote
I depict
I deploy
I describe
I deserve
I design
I designate

I desire
I detect
I determine
I develop
I diagnose
I dialogue
I dictate
I digest
I dignify
I direct
I discover
I discuss
I dispense
I display
I dispose
I distinguish
I distribute
I diversify
I divine
I do
I document
I draw
I dream
I dress
I drive
I drum
I dwell

- E -
I earn
I eat
I edify
I educate
I educe
I effect

I elaborate
I elate
I elect
I elevate
I elicit
I emanate
I emancipate
I embark
I embellish
I embody
I embrace
I emerge
I emit
I emograph
I emote
I empathize
I employ
I empower
I emulate
I enchant
I encounter
I encourage
I endeavor
I endorse
I endure
I engage
I engender
I engineer
I engrave
I engross
I enhance
I enhearten
I enjoy
I enlighten
I enliven
I ennoble

I enrich
I enroll
I ensure
I enter
I entertain
I enthrall
I enthrone
I enthuse
I entice
I enunciate
I envision
I equalize
I erect
I escort
I espouse
I establish
I esteem
I estimate
I eternize
I evoke
I evolve
I exact
I examine
I excel
I exchange
I excite
I exclaim
I execute
I exercise
I exert
I exhale
I exhibit
I exhilarate
I exhort
I exist
I exit

I expand
I expect
I expectorate
I expedite
I experience
I experiment
I explain
I explicate
I explore
I export
I expose
I express
I extend
I extinguish
I extract
I extrapolate
I exuberate
I exult

- F -
I familiarize
I fancy
I fantasize
I farm
I fashion
I fasten
I father
I favor
I feast
I feature
I feed
I feel
I felicitate
I fellowship
I feminize

I fertilize
I figure
I file
I fill
I finance
I find
I finish
I fish
I fit
I fix
I flavor
I flex
I float
I flourish
I flow
I flower
I fly
I focus
I follow
I footnote
I forecast
I foresee
I foretell
I forgive
I form
I format
I formulate
I franchise
I fraternize
I free
I frequent
I freshen
I fructify
I fulfill
I function
I furnish

I further
I fuse

I gain
I galvanize
I game
I gargle
I garnish
I gather
I gauge
I gaze
I generate
I gesticulate
I gesture
I get
I gift
I giggle
I gild
I give
I glamorize
I gleam
I glorify
I go
I govern
I grace
I graduate
I grant
I graph
I grasp
I greet
I grieve
I grin
I grip
I groom
I groove

I ground
I group
I grow
I grub
I guarantee
I guard
I guide

- H -
I habituate
I handle
I happen
I harmonize
I harp
I harvest
I have
I head
I headline
I heal
I hear
I hearten
I heat
I heed
I help
I hire
I hold
I honor
I hope
I host
I hostess
I hum
I humor
I hurry
I hustle
I hydrate

- I -
I ideate
I identify
I illuminate
I illustrate
I imagine
I imbibe
I implement
I import
I impress
I improve
I improvise
I incarnate
I incline
I include
I increase
I indulge
I infer
I influence
I inform
I ingratiate
I inhale
I inherit
I initiate
I input
I inquire
I insert
I insist
I inspect
I inspire
I install
I institute
I instruct
I insure
I integrate
I intend

I intercede
I interpret
I intervene
I interview
I intimate
I intone
I intuit
I invent
I invest
I invite

- J -
I jam
I jazz
I join
I joke
I journal
I juggle
I juice
I jump

- K -
I keep
I ken
I kiss
I know

- L -
I labor
I land
I landscape
I last
I laud
I laugh
I launch
I launder

I lead
I learn
I leave
I lecture
I let
I level
I levitate
I liberate
I license
I like
I listen
I live
I locate
I look
I love
I lunch
I lure
I luxuriate
I lyricize

- M -
I magnetize
I magnify
I maintain
I make
I make-believe
I make-up
I make-up-my-mind
I manage
I maneuver
I manifest
I manipulate
I manufacture
I manuscript
I map

I marathon
I marry
I marvel
I masculinize
I massage
I master
I match
I mate
I materialize
I matriculate
I matrix
I matter
I maturate
I mature
I maximize
I may
I mean
I measure
I mechanize
I mediate
I meditate
I meet
I memorize
I mend
I mention
I mentor
I merchandize
I merit
I merry make
I mesh
I mesmerize
I metabolize
I metamorphose
I might
I mind
I mingle

I minimize
I minister
I mirror
I mitigate
I mix
I mobilize
I model
I moderate
I modernize
I modify
I modulate
I moisten
I mold
I mollify
I moralize
I mother
I motivate
I move
I mull
I multiply
I muse
I must
I mutate
I mutualize

- N -
I name
I navigate
I need
I negotiate
I nest
I net
I network
I nominate
I notate
I notice

I notify
I nourish
I number
I numerate
I nurture

- O -
I observe
I obtain
I obviate
I occupy
I occur
I offer
I ogle
I open
I open sesame
I operate
I optimize
I option
I orbit
I orchestrate
I order
I organize
I orientate
I originate
I osculate
I oust
I out think
I outgo
I outline
I outshine
I own
I oxygenate
I oxygenize

- P -
I pace make
I pacify
I paint
I pair
I palpate
I pantomime
I paraphrase
I pardon
I parent
I partake
I participate
I partner
I party
I patent
I pattern
I peace make
I pedal
I peg
I pen
I pencil
I perceive
I perform
I perfume
I permit
I perpetuate
I persevere
I persist
I personalize
I personify
I persuade
I peruse
I pervade
I pet
I petition
I phase

I philosophize
I phonate
I photograph
I phrase
I pick
I picket
I picture
I pierce
I pilot
I pioneer
I place
I plan
I plant
I play
I play write
I please
I pleasure
I plow
I ploy
I plug
I plumb
I plunge
I ply
I poetize
I point
I poise
I polarize
I polish
I ponder
I popularize
I populate
I portent
I portion
I portray
I pose
I position

I post
I postulate
I posture
I potentiate
I pounce
I pound
I pour
I practice
I praise
I prance
I pray
I precede
I predict
I preface
I prefer
I preform
I prelude
I premeditate
I premiere
I prepare
I present
I preserve
I press
I pretend
I prevent
I preview
I print
I prioritize
I prize
I process
I proclaim
I procure
I produce
I profess
I profit

I program
I progress
I project
I proliferate
I prologue
I prolong
I promenade
I promise
I promote
I prompt
I promulgate
I pronounce
I pronunciate
I proof read
I prop
I propel
I prophesy
I proportion
I propose
I prospect
I protagonize
I protect
I prototype
I protract
I prove
I provide
I prune
I publicize
I publish
I pull
I pulsate
I pun
I punctuate
I purchase
I purge
I purify

I purport
I purpose
I pursue
I put
I puzzle

- Q -
I quadrate
I quadruple
I quaff
I qualify
I quantify
I quench
I query
I quest
I question
I quicken
I quieten
I quilt
I quiz
I quote

- R -
I race
I radiate
I rain
I raise
I rally
I reach
I read
I realize
I reap
I rear
I reason
I reassure
I rebound

I recall
I receive
I reciprocate
I recite
I reckon
I reclaim
I recline
I recognize
I recollect
I recommend
I recompense
I reconcile
I reconstruct
I record
I recount
I recoup
I recover
I recreate
I refer
I refine
I reflect
I refresh
I regale
I regard
I regenerate
I register
I regulate
I rehearse
I reign
I reiterate
I rejoice
I rejuvenate
I relate
I relax
I relieve

I relish
I remain
I remark
I remember
I remind
I remit
I render
I rendezvous
I renew
I repair
I repeat
I repel
I represent
I request
I require
I reserve
I reside
I resile
I resolve
I resonate
I resound
I resource
I respect
I respire
I respond
I rest
I restore
I restrict
I result
I resume
I resurge
I resurrect
I resuscitate
I retail
I retain
I reticulate

I retreat
I retrieve
I return
I reveal
I revel
I review
I revise
I revive
I reward
I rewrite
I rhyme
I riddle
I ride
I right
I ring
I rinse
I ripen
I ripple
I rise
I roam
I roast
I robe
I rock
I rocket
I roll
I romance
I romp
I roof
I room
I root
I rose
I rotate
I rouse
I route
I row
I rub

I rule
I ruminate
I run

- S -
I sail
I salivate
I salsa
I salvage
I sample
I sand
I sanitize
I satisfy
I sauté
I save
I savor
I savvy
I saw
I say
I scaffold
I scale
I scent
I schedule
I scheme
I school
I scintillate
I scoop
I scoot
I score
I scour
I scout
I scramble
I scrape
I scratch
I screen

I scribe
I script
I scrub
I scrutinize
I sculpt
I search
I season
I seat
I second
I secrete
I section
I secure
I see
I seed
I seek
I seem
I segment
I segue
I select
I sell
I send
I sense
I separate
I serenade
I serialize
I serve
I set
I settle
I sew
I shade
I shall
I shampoo
I shape
I share
I shed
I shelter

I shelve
I shepherd
I shield
I shift
I shine
I ship
I shoe
I shoo
I shoot
I shop
I shoulder
I shout
I show
I shower
I shut
I shuttle
I sift
I sight
I sign
I signal
I signify
I simplify
I sing
I single
I sit
I situate
I size
I skate
I sketch
I slake
I slate
I sleep
I slenderize
I smell
I smile
I smooth

I sniff
I snuggle
I soak
I soar
I socialize
I solace
I solicit
I solve
I soothe
I sort
I sound
I span
I spare
I spark
I sparkle
I speak
I specialize
I specify
I speculate
I spell
I spend
I spice
I spin
I spiral
I spirit
I sponsor
I spoon
I sport
I spot
I spread
I spring
I sprinkle
I sprout
I square
I squeeze

I squire
I stabilize
I stack
I staff
I stage
I stamp
I stand
I star
I start
I state
I stay
I steady
I steer
I stem
I step
I sterilize
I steward
I stipulate
I stir
I stitch
I stock
I stop
I store
I strengthen
I stretch
I stride
I string
I strive
I stroke
I structure
I strum
I study
I style
I stylize
I submerge
I submit

I subrogate
I subscribe
I subsist
I substitute
I subsume
I succeed
I suggest
I summarize
I summer
I summon
I sun
I sup
I supervise
I supplement
I supply
I support
I suppose
I surmise
I surmount
I surpass
I surprise
I survey
I survive
I suspend
I sustain
I swallow
I swap
I sweep
I swim
I swing
I swirl
I syllogize
I symphonize
I synchronize
I syncopate
I syncretize

I synergize
I synthesize
I systemize

- T -
I tabulate
I tackle
I talk
I tape
I taste
I teach
I team
I tell
I temper
I term
I terminate
I test
I testify
I texture
I thank
I thank you!
I theorize
I think
I thirst
I thought
I thread
I thrill
I throw
I thumb
I tickle
I tidy
I tie
I time
I tip
I tithe

I tolerate
I touch
I toy
I trace
I train
I transcend
I transcribe
I transfer
I transform

I translate
I transmit
I transpire
I transport
I transpose
I travel
I tread
I treasure
I treat
I trinitize
I triumph
I trust
I tune
I turn
I tutor
I twist
I type

- U -
I underscore
I undersign
I understand
I understudy
I undertake
I underwrite
I undo

I unfold
I unite
I update
I uphold
I uplift
I urge
I use
I utilize
I utter

- V -
I vacation
I validate
I value
I venerate
I venture
I verbalize
I verify
I vibrate
I view
I vindicate
I vision
I visit
I visualize
I vitalize
I vivify
I vocalize
I voice

I volunteer
I vouch
I voyage

- W -
I wake
I walk
I waltz
I want
I warm
I warrant
I wash
I watch
I water
I wave
I weave
I weed
I welcome
I whisper
I whistle
I will
I win
I wind
I wink
I winter
I wire
I wish
I witness

I wonder
I word
I work
I worship
I would
I wrap
I wriggle
I write

- X -
I Xerox
I x-ray

- Y -
I yea
I yearn
I yield
I yoke
I yoo-hoo

- Z -
I zero
I zest
I zip
I zone
I zoom

Dictionary Legend

adj. – adjective
n. - noun
syn. - synonym
v. - verb
v.i. – verb intransitive
v.t. – verb transitive

For further definitions
please refer to your favorite dictionary!

About the Author

BeBe hails from Maryland yet calls Colorado home. Second eldest of ten children, she's forged, from years of observation, a method of rearing young that can be celebrated as a momentous break-through in behavior modification. Using simple tools from the English language she's designed a system free from politics, free from religion and free from any agenda other than to teach the child how to think for itself and become the best it can become.

In writing this book, her main concerns were to help others in developing improved (1) self-confidence, (2) communication skills, (3) people skills, (4) leadership skills, and (5) skills for controlling stress.

A natural storyteller, BeBe speaks to various groups in the Denver, Metro area and people entranced by listening to her stories of possibilities. To rapt audiences, she richly details her journey of writing The Be Attitudes with humor and honest reflection, the good times and the hardships. She tells how she took on the challenge of a life-long dream and learned quickly how to adapt to a swiftly changing world always living on the edge of her comfort zone.

Invite your audience to learn how using everyday words can get whatever they want... and in the meanwhile learn how to breathe like a dolphin. Sometime serious, sometimes funny, always inspirational, BeBe's program personifies the spirit of identity, commitment and perseverance compelling each to follow the road to their wildest dreams... one step at a time. And, she'll play her banjo for you if you ask real nice.

She's available for book signings, book readings and speaking at public events... simply email her at this email address: be@bebe.bz with the subject heading: Booking BeBe Dept. Or contact her at the publisher.

**A portion of the proceeds
from sales of this book go to sponsor**

Project Cause

∞

www.firethegrid.org

Look for these other fine books by BeBe

* Breathing Like A Dolphin - Hyperbaric Medicine at Home.

* Your Spiritual Birthday

Soon to be at www.BeBe.Bz

You are hereby invited
to submit comments, testimonials and suggestions
"No-strings-attached" by mail to:

Be Be
P. O. Box 140661
Edgewater, Colorado 80214
USA

Or visit on line at www.TheBeAttitudes.com

Also – sign up to receive Positive Attitudes Daily
via email at www.TheDailyAttitude.com

Gift others with both
The Be Attitudes and The Daily Attitude.